With L... ...
a

Healing Grief,
Finding Peace

Healing Grief, *Finding Peace*

101 WAYS TO COPE WITH THE DEATH OF YOUR LOVED ONE

DR. LOUIS E. LAGRAND
Foreword by Kenneth J. Doka, PhD

Copyright © 2011 by Louis LaGrand
Cover and internal design © 2011 by Sourcebooks, Inc.
Cover design by Cyanotype Book Architects
Cover image © Barcin/iStockphoto.com

Sourcebooks and the colophon are registered trademarks of Sourcebooks, Inc.

All rights reserved. No part of this book may be reproduced in any form or by any electronic or mechanical means including information storage and retrieval systems— except in the case of brief quotations embodied in critical articles or reviews—without permission in writing from its publisher, Sourcebooks, Inc.

This publication is designed to provide accurate and authoritative information in regard to the subject matter covered. It is sold with the understanding that the publisher is not engaged in rendering legal, accounting, or other professional service. If legal advice or other expert assistance is required, the services of a competent professional person should be sought.—*From a Declaration of Principles Jointly Adopted by a Committee of the American Bar Association and a Committee of Publishers and Associations*

This book is not intended as a substitute for medical advice from a qualified physician. The intent of this book is to provide accurate general information in regard to the subject matter covered. If medical advice or other expert help is needed, the services of an appropriate medical professional should be sought.

All brand names and product names used in this book are trademarks, registered trademarks, or trade names of their respective holders. Sourcebooks, Inc., is not associated with any product or vendor in this book.

Published by Sourcebooks, Inc.
P.O. Box 4410, Naperville, Illinois 60567-4410
(630) 961-3900
Fax: (630) 961-2168
www.sourcebooks.com

Library of Congress Cataloging-in-Publication Data

LaGrand, Louis E.
  Healing grief, finding peace : 101 ways to cope with the death of your loved one / by Louis E. LaGrand.
    p. cm.
  Includes bibliographical references.
  (pbk. : alk. paper) 1. Bereavement—Psychological aspects. 2. Death—Psychological aspects. 3. Grief. I. Title.
  BF575.G7L337 2011
  155.9'37—dc23

                        2011031247

Printed and bound in the United States.
VP 10 9 8 7 6 5 4 3

Dedicated to all who are mourning and all who must inevitably respond to the opposite side of the coin of love.

The best thing for being sad is to learn something. That is the only thing that never fails.

—T.H. White in The Once and Future King

Act as if what you do makes a difference. It does.

—William James

Contents

Foreword

We have no choice about grief. No one asks if this is a convenient time for someone we love to die. We have no choice in that we will react to that loss. Our reactions may be intense and consuming or, perhaps, more muted. Our grief may be expressed in the ways that we feel or think about our loved one, or in how we behave. Our grief may even affect us spiritually or physically. We have no choice as to whether we will react—that is a given.

We do have choices, however, in how we cope with our grief—on how we adapt to the loss, however horrible, that we experienced. That is the gift of Dr. Louis LaGrand's book, *Healing Grief, Finding Peace*. Dr. LaGrand offers a plethora of ideas, proven over time, which will help us even as we deal with grief. He speaks from great experience. For over thirty years, Dr. LaGrand has been a pioneer in the study of grief. He has not only taught, researched, and written about grief, he is also a counselor. His advice and recommendations reach from and to both heart and head.

As we read these recommendations, it is important to maintain our own personal prism, our own lens. LaGrand offers a buffet of ideas—some of them will be suitable, while others may not necessarily resonate. That's the joy of this book. With a hundred ideas and suggestions, we will be sure to find much that satisfies and nourishes us as we journey with grief.

Many of LaGrand's suggestions are solid fare. The first half of LaGrand's presentation suggests we learn about grief, understand and validate our feelings, and proactively respond to them. We know, for example, that certain days such as holidays and birthdays will be difficult. We need to understand that we can plan for them—reflecting on who we want to be with, how we want to spend the day, and what we wish and need to do. This section is the meat and potatoes of LaGrand's book.

The next half includes more subtle suggestions. LaGrand is sensitive to all the current trends in contemporary grief theory. He understands that we never give up our relationship with the person who died, that we continue to maintain a bond. In fact, his earlier work on the extraordinary ways that we experience the presence of the deceased through dreams, visions, olfactory experiences (such as smelling her perfume), symbolic experiences, or synchronicities underlies that notion that we never lose a connection. Rituals, memorials, and symbolic mementoes can all offer reminders of that continuing connection.

LaGrand is responsive as well to all the losses that can generate grief and shows particular sensitivity to the techniques that disenfranchised grievers—that is, those who have losses unacknowledged by others—can use to effectively cope with grief.

Most importantly, LaGrand understands a powerful and important lesson about grief—that even in grief, we can still grow.

Certain experiences, my godson once reminded me, leave you only two choices—to grow up or to grow down. Loss and grief are such experiences. As we cope with our loss, we may gain new insights and different perspectives, or cultivate new skills. We may have an enhanced understanding of the power and importance of relationships or the fragility of life that leads to a renewed appreciation of life, even in loss. We can, as my godson said, grow up. That too is one of our choices.

Kenneth J. Doka, PhD
Professor, The Graduate School, The College of New Rochelle
Senior Consultant, Hospice Foundation of America

Acknowledgments

A book about managing grief is essentially one built on the wisdom of those who have gone before us. I am especially indebted to all who I have been privileged to serve. You have taught me so much through the years and also helped me understand that each of us possesses the strength that lies deep within to deal with the most difficult losses imaginable.

I deeply appreciate and thank each of you for sharing your feelings and thoughts with me and helping me realize that grief is a part of life that causes us to examine our beliefs and expectations. This examination consistently results in developing a new awareness and growth as we adapt.

I also wish to thank everyone who has read various portions of the manuscript and offered valuable advice. Ben Wolfe, Delpha Camp, Jane Bissler, Chris Duminiak, and Tom Toolen I deeply appreciate the time and energy you willingly gave in shaping the final product.

A special thanks goes out to Ken Doka, a long-time colleague, who so willingly has shared his knowledge about grief with thousands of people throughout the world. His skills as a therapist are of the highest quality.

And finally, I thank Kelly Bale my editor at Sourcebooks. You are truly an outstanding professional and your suggestions have been, without question, a great contribution.

First Words:
How You Can Ease the
Hurt and Heartache

To him who is determined it remains only to act.

—ITALIAN PROVERB

Time heals all wounds" is an often quoted message of hope given to those mourning the death of a loved one. Regrettably, it is a half-truth at best. As a wise mother whose seventeen-year-old son was killed in an automobile accident said to me: "Time only heals if you work between the minutes." By working between the minutes, you change your relationship to your great loss, see it from a different perspective, and realize that love lasts forever. The chain of love—the relationship—is never broken.

This book is all about working between the minutes to solve the problems of restarting life without your loved one. The work of adjustment is inescapable. The change you wish to see—especially the reduction of pain—never takes place by looking outside of yourself; transformation occurs only by looking within, *altering perceptions and the quality of your inner life.*

The 101 coping strategies presented here are specific, how-to oriented approaches that ultimately give you pathways for achieving lasting inner peace by using the one thing you can control—your responses.

Accommodating what comes into your life—whether you like it or not—is a major factor in peaceful living. The renowned English novelist Virginia Woolf put it this way: "Arrange whatever pieces come your way." Critical advice! Resistance to change, refusing to arrange the pieces, *always* brings more inner conflict and pain than grief naturally allowed to unfold, because you are interfering with a normal process. *No one controls change.*

Knowing what you can and cannot control can go a long way toward preventing and reducing depression. Death shatters our illusion that we are actually in control. Grief has always been an experience that presents the opportunity to redefine ourselves and our world and find new meaning, value, and vision for our lives. Surrender is a critical part of that transformation.

There are many ways to cope with big losses as you will discover in the pages ahead. You can reach acceptance by taking small, loving, time-consuming steps in the right direction. I strongly urge you to take your time and carefully read each coping suggestion. You cannot do them all, *but you can pick and choose what seems right for you.* Some will be most useful early in your grief, others later, when you feel stronger. You decide when your heart tells you it's time.

And if you start crying when reading, put the book down, cry freely, and come back later. But be sure to let the tears flow. You don't have to start with chapter 1 if you'd rather not. Look at the table of contents and decide where you want to go and what coping strategy you want to access first. Read with a red pencil in hand. When something hits you in a positive way, underline it or put a check mark next to it. This will make it easier to review each week, which we all need to do from time to time, as it is easy to forget, especially when stressed. Try not to rush looking for a sudden solution to take away the pain. None exists.

Make notes in the margins when reading to capture new ideas that will pop into your mind, especially when I pose questions. Take advantage of these thoughts so they don't slip away; they come from a good place within you. Later on, as you review them, they will become treasured resources and you can more easily remember what you want to accomplish. And be sure to stop during your reading and mull over what you just read. Think about how you can apply the idea to your situation. When you have a bad day, go back and read the sections you have underlined.

The pivotal consideration is: you have to decide where you will begin your journey, where you will take the first step in the process of integrating your great loss into life. In essence, you must make the first noticeable move and believe healthy mourning is possible.

• • •

For over thirty years I have helped the bereaved in a variety of settings—hospices, hospitals, support groups, and individual counseling. I was one of the founders and President of the Board of Directors of Hospice and Palliative Care of the St. Lawrence Valley, possess three graduate degrees, including a PhD, and have worked with hundreds of mourners. I have often heard the bereaved tell their stories of how they dealt with their great losses. I have listened to many colleagues talk about coping with the big losses in life and was a board member of the Association for Death Education and Counseling, for whom I have given numerous presentations on grief at their annual conferences.

Significantly, I am no stranger to great loss, having suffered the deaths of my parents, an older brother and a younger sister, and, most demandingly, the death of my only daughter. My wife and I found Karen dead in her crib one hot August afternoon. It was, to say the least, a major assault on our senses and our views of life.

I tell you this so you will know as you read this book that I have experienced the grief of clients, as well as in my own personal life. I have some inkling—only a tiny bit—of how you must feel. I say a tiny bit, because no one can ever know how you really feel based on *their own* experiences. Only you know the depths of your grief, since every relationship, like a fingerprint, is one of a kind. That is why family members often grieve quite differently from each other. In truth, there are as many grieving styles as there are lifestyles and each family member's way needs to be respected. How we grieve depends on the complex nature of our relationship to the loved one and our past experiences with loss. For example, my wife carried Karen within herself for nine months and took care of her much more, as I was in graduate school at the time of her death. Our different relationships with her, as well as ingrained cultural influences, caused us to grieve Karen's loss in unique ways.

Do You Know Your Grieving Style?

Let's begin by looking at your grieving style. Coping strategies are both behavioral and psychological, focusing on problem-solving and regulating the emotional consequences of loss. Although men and women tend to grieve in one style more than another, they also possess many similarities. Generally, women are more expressive and emotive, what experts call intuitive grievers. Men are said to be instrumental grievers and immerse themselves in doing things; they internally process the loss, as so-called silent grievers, showing little emotion.

Of course, these descriptions are an oversimplification, since each of us has both male and female genes and use *both* instrumental and intuitive ways to grieve. This is important to understand. A wide mixture of action-oriented grieving occurs among both sexes, where some individuals possess more expressive characteristics, need to do more things, and yet also work internally to process their feelings.

Where do you stand? What are your needs? What do you want?

Your answers to these three questions will be of immense help in coping with your loss—especially the last one. The path you choose to heal will be uniquely your own, featuring what you want. In other words, what do you want to do with your changed life? What do you want to do with your grief? What are your *goals* in adapting to your great loss? How do you wish to relate to your loved one? Knowing what you want is not an insignificant question; it is the prelude to coping well and raises you to greater awareness and a higher level of existence. Try to become aware, as soon as possible, of what you need to do to process and express your grief, and how you want to be helped. Significant differences exist among grievers, especially in those around you, and all are "right" for each individual. Don't get caught up in worrying about what is the "appropriate" way to grieve for your gender. Let go of all stereotypes.

Yes, men often have certain "stiff upper lip" characteristics and women certain outgoing and effusive ones that lead them to wisely look for support. However, this doesn't mean that some individuals may not experience opposite grieving styles. Bottom line: Your personal style dictates the degrees to which you will cope intuitively (expressing much feeling) or instrumentally (more actively doing) or a combination of both. For all practical purposes, you will do some of both. And that's good. Just become aware of your style.

Ways to Heal

I have used many of the tools and strategies presented in this book to deal with the numerous changes in my life, whether it was a loss from physical death, a financial setback, a move away, a growing up, or a falling out, and have also recommended them to those I have counseled. These strategies succeed, when you make the effort to work with them rather than expect immediate relief, as we have been conditioned to believe is possible.

Are there some "one-minute wonders"? Yes, some things help immediately; however, they are few and far between. Changes most often happen when you make them in small manageable pieces. It is your never-give-up grief work that pays off. The emphasis is on work, the painful confrontation with the reality of the loss in your style of adapting to change. Whatever your style, you must *rise* to the next level.

How? Let me explain.

Focus On Words with Authority

Words shape thoughts, attitudes, actions, and how you cope with loss. In short, they shape your reality. Part of coping well has a lot to do with the words you repetitively feed yourself. Your thoughts, a superior resource, create the direction you will travel. Choice is an expression of your greatest power, and you will hear me talk about it

> Grief work is commonly defined by counselors as the labor required in coming to terms with or adapting to the loss of a loved one.

throughout the book. You can choose words to help accomplish whatever you want. Choice demands that you consciously feature the "D" word, *determination*, in your belief system. Here is the single most influential decision you can make to jump-start the journey through loss. Be determined that you will acknowledge nothing less than to adapt to the new circumstances of your life. Make the "D" word the cornerstone of your new life.

Vigorous determination, at some point in the process of grieving, is a commitment you can make. This may seem too simplistic for you. But all successful loss management begins with how we think. A deep, driving desire, a 100 percent commitment, has worked for millions and it will work for you. Your conscious decision to be determined to prevail—a decision you renew every day on rising—is the keystone to coping well.

How do you become determined?

Find a reason greater than yourself to change your motivation and the determination buried deep inside waiting for your call will awake; it is part of the free will everyone possesses. Think of what you love or have a passion for. Your spirituality, your children, your students, your legacy, your skills and experiences to pass on to others, or your desire to be more fully present to all you come in contact with are starters to consider. Think about your deceased loved one as the reason. He or she would want you to have a good life for his or her sake. Keep that reason alive in your heart.

Convince yourself that you are going to win this difficult struggle by doing the best you can. Start right away. Don't put this inner conversation off any longer. You already have all you need to get started. As the proverb opening this introduction suggests, determination and action are potent stuff.

Utilize Your Unconscious Mind

Your unconscious is a priceless resource that goes largely untapped when mourning the death of a loved one. Yet, it will always unknowingly help bring what you want to bear in action—if you realize that your conscious mind is in charge of what goes into the unconscious. This implies the necessity to avoid distorted or emotion-laden stimuli as much as possible. Not an easy job.

Obviously, monitoring the types of thought patterns you allow to dominate your daily inner monologue will either enhance or destroy your efforts to face difficult changes. There is no middle ground here. Becoming an expert in what you let in and let go of is a sure-fire way to feel better. Influence the unconscious by always communicating with it through the use of the powerful "I am," as in:

> I am determined to persist.
> I am doing difficult tasks every day without fail.
> I am a committed and powerful human being.
> I am making it.
> I am good.
> I am divinely guided and assisted.
> I am getting it done.

Use whatever words are authoritative for you; they are powerful ways to dispel fear. Try not to take your internal monologue lightly—it chatters constantly, has powerful consequences, and can hurt as well as help as directed. I use the word "power" here and throughout the book to mean "ability" or "potential," not as any form of coercion.

The above "I am" statements are also considered to be verbal reframes. A reframe is a process in which you consciously change meaning or perspective on a situation. Reframes highly influence beliefs because they create a shift in consciousness. Beliefs affect judgment and emotional responses and control behavior. If you so desire, you can reframe any situation and be the better for doing so. It is an extremely significant coping technique.

TRY THIS

For a first line of self-care, try writing specific inspiring phrases you have created on a 3" by 5" card that you can whip out and read when you start feeling the blues or are alone on a trip. I ask every mourner I work with to memorize the following sentence from the poem "Will" by American author and poet Ella Wheeler Wilcox: "There is no chance, no destiny, no fate, can circumvent or hinder or control the firm resolve of a determined soul."

Maintain a Plan B

Always have an alternative plan for when those big waves of grief become overwhelming, you run into a bad day, or realize that some people are expecting you to follow their agenda for your grief work. Utilize one of the stress-release techniques outlined in this book as a way to deal with the additional stress overload. Then, as you get through another day, keep telling yourself you are capable of getting through the next long, dark night. You will discover your coping skills and inherent ability to manage loss, as you experience grief.

Accept what is. We age quickly or gracefully depending on our emotional reactions to the events in life. Recognize that no one escapes getting into a "negative" state. It's part of life. Yet a constant negative emotional life is unhealthy for the brain, hastens the aging process, contributes to a host of degenerative diseases, and *attracts more stress*. Equally important, gale-force negativity promotes ineffective coping strategies. But you can change all this.

It is healthy to look back and reminisce about your loved one, yet it is crucial that as soon as possible you spend much more time *focusing on the present* and directions to take for the future. Those who cope well and adapt to massive change have learned how to deal with the new conditions of their lives, paying more attention to the present moment. At the same time, you still build a new relationship with the person who died by learning to love in separation through memories, traditions, spirit, and in lessons learned.

Avoid the trap of spending so much time in the past that you become mired in it and cannot reach the major goal of grieving: *acceptance of the reality of your loss*. This means recognizing a view of life that includes the unthinkable—an awareness that life will be new and different without the physical presence of our loved one. Or, put in behavioral terms, being able to talk and think about your loved one without emotional pain.

Acceptance of what *is* will enable you to more freely construct how to integrate your loss into life. You have no power to change what happened. You have to own it as a part of your history. Owning life as it unfolds is the true and only route to healing and eventually to finding satisfaction and meaning once again. Yet it takes time and much struggle. Without striving to attain it, your pain will be impossible to manage.

The Power of Negative Thoughts

The most difficult enemies you will encounter on your way to finding peace are the ones that live within. Nothing begins without a thought. First, be aware that we all have negative thoughts and painful feelings that pop up at various times. And there is no proven method to dispatch them permanently so that you never experience them again. That said, negative thoughts are just as powerful as positive ones; both spread good or bad (and draining) energy within and to those around you. But negative thoughts can be intercepted and managed. How? Like all other skills—through practicing a specific positive change.

Most negative thoughts are not true and cannot hold up under scrutiny. Yet, on any given day, you will allow more negative thoughts to dominate—upward of 70 percent of all thoughts, say experts—unless you decide to limit their freedom to roam around inside. This is where you can prevail. If you constantly think that you can't get through your ordeal, you are assured to have a prolonged painful experience.

Why?

Because thoughts have the power to draw within or repel more of the same. Thoughts are mind-habits, and part of your grief work is to establish new mind-habits. This means challenging thoughts that are untrue. Deny the negative power of "I can't," or any other negative statement, to live rent-free in your head. Keep holding the way you want to cope in your thoughts, put the thoughts into action, and that is exactly what you will eventually bring to pass.

Ultimately, with your thought focus, you have to install an alternate *behavior* pattern and stop reinforcing what you don't want.

Fight consistently to squash ANTs (automatic negative thoughts), which have a home in your unconscious mind. They are not only relationship killers—they foster depression, lead to scary dreams, and add severely to your physical woes. "Wisdom," observed Dr. Wayne Dyer, world-renowned speaker, author, and psychotherapist, "is avoiding all thoughts that weaken you." So become aware of your negative patterns of thinking and intervene.

Your Ultimate Goal— Embracing Your New Life

Now here is the taproot pivotal question that arises insistently and begs to be asked:

Will you be loss-oriented in the months and years ahead—or will you be restoration-oriented?

Will you maintain your bitter primary focus on loss, or give more time to rebuilding? Put another way, are you going to allow the death of your loved one to define you? Reread the first question and think long and hard on the consequences of your decision. Good grief means realizing you cannot completely eliminate inner thoughts of sadness, but instead establish new habits to take away the power of sad thoughts to overwhelm and destroy.

For most of us, thinking about a new life without our loved one is absolutely absurd. We've lost ourselves, are on autopilot, and long for the security of the familiar, but in reality, we ultimately have to build a new life without the many interactions that used to occur when our loved one was with us. You have a decision to make here: you can be in charge of how you want this life to unfold, or you can haphazardly let it be fashioned. In any event, it will occur, one way or the other; it is inevitable. A new life will start for you, and here's why:

- Life has changed without your loved one and you have to develop new daily habits of living. This is a major part of grief work. Make a list of your new routines (not an easy task to accomplish) and force yourself to repeatedly make the difficult transitions. Stepping into the unknown is risky, but taking the calculated risk is what coping well entails.
- Your identity is altered, even though you don't want it to be. You are not the same person, and some of your friends will relate to you differently. Redefining ourselves, that is, building a new identity after the death of a loved one, is another significant task commonly forgotten in grief work. It's okay to be a different person than when you started your journey through loss. So ask yourself how much your great loss has affected your identity as a person and how you will rebuild it.
- Identity formation is not an early task of grief, and you may not be ready to take it seriously now. Reestablishing identity takes much time and effort: you have to mull over who you are now

and what you want (your goals). You have the right to choose how and how much you need to change over time.

- A part of you has died, that part which interacted with a major source of your nurturing community. Counselors call it the death of the interactional self. You can learn various ways to fill that void.
- You may have to develop new skills, interests, and abilities or change your role in the family to assume the responsibilities of the loved one who died. As Gandhi once said, "You must be the change you wish to see in the world."

If you open yourself to the concept of a new life and partial identity change, you open yourself to new opportunities, new experiences, and new possibilities. These are all strategic moves forward. You can win the internal struggle to build a new life, when you decide it's time. No one knows when you will start the task. Yet each of us has the innate capacity to deal with these new circumstances and adapt to the unfamiliar. We are built to conquer change, which always dogs us, even though the process brings out our fear of the unknown.

We can't do anything about what has happened, but we can do so much about how we will handle our misery. This is what doing your grief work is all about. Surrender to your new life. The former nun Joan Chittister writes in *Scarred by Struggle, Transformed by Hope*: "Surrender does not mean that I quit grieving what I do not have. It means I surrender to new meanings and new circumstances."

Of course, this is easy to say, but surrendering is an uphill struggle. But you can do it too, though you may not think so at this time. You are more than you think you are. There are many tried and true ways that will get you through the difficult journey. You will discover ways to manage loss that others have used, that will save you loads of unnecessary suffering. That is another goal of this book—to minimize unnecessary suffering in meeting the challenge of dealing with the changes you will face.

In *Healing Grief, Finding Peace*, we will explore:

- the most overlooked factor in coping with the death of a loved one;
- the difference between grieving and healing;
- inner-strength healing strategies (working between your ears);
- other-centered healing strategies (reaching out to heal); and
- little-used but highly effective healing strategies.

In each of these areas, you will find a wealth of information to help you through the challenging days ahead, and to take the action needed to accept your great loss at the heart level. Take what you can use for now; let go of the rest for a later time. You may have to release some old assumptions and beliefs about loss (most of us do) and step forward each day to create your new life. That will make the difference between coping well and sabotaging yourself with unnecessary emotional pain.

To sum up, how can you reconcile your loss and reduce the hurt?

- Form the intention right now that you want to integrate your loss into life, as impossible as that might seem. The power of consistent intention is grossly underestimated, yet it is the starting point for any progress in adapting. Set your intention every morning before getting out of bed.
- Develop some of the survival and growth skills you read about in the chapters ahead.
- Begin today to learn to love in separation. More about that later.

If you are ready, let's begin the task of gaining heart acceptance and help answer the key questions that surround all loss experiences.

ONE

What You Need to Know about Grief and Healing

When we do the best that we can, we never know what miracle is wrought in our life, or in the life of another.

—HELEN KELLER

S ince loss is a condition of existence, the grief that follows it is automatic as well. But let me tell you this: you can eventually camouflage it, as many do, in hopes that you won't be avoided by people whom you normally interact with. However, loads of research studies show that keeping these feelings of loss within has a major detrimental effect on the physical body and lengthens the time it takes to adapt.

WHAT IS THE DIFFERENCE BETWEEN GRIEVING AND HEALING?

Everyone grieves—there is no escape—but not everyone heals; they believe they can't adapt to or share the pain. Many relive their grief on a continuous basis. Yet, grief is the **normal** inner response to the loss of a valued person or object. It usually, though not always, includes a host of emotions like anger, guilt, depression or despair, denial, feelings of failure, and feeling misunderstood by friends and family. You might think that you are falling apart and that nothing will help. You are out of control. Waves of total insecurity seem to sweep over you, and you question if you will be able to make it. And there may be occasions when you feel nothing at all. You are numb. Or you may panic, caught in an emotional swamp.

What is important to realize is that the appearance of some or all of these emotions (and many more), at various times, is entirely normal. We expect these emotions to surface when someone loved is suddenly absent from our surroundings and we feel unfairly deprived. The feelings of confusion or frustration may be overwhelming, yet everyone has emotional wounds in life. Everyone. They can be worked through if you recognize them for what they are: signals to reassess the direction of your grief work and thoughts on your new life without your loved one.

Healing centers on opening yourself to the support of others and sharing what is happening inside with them. *Telling your story to trusted others is a major part of healing and adapting to change.* In the process, the meaning of your story becomes clearer. Healing always involves interpersonal relationships that are vehicles for absorbing emotion. Others may influence the way we perceive our grief, sometimes having a negative effect. The right support persons give us needed emotional safety. Seek out those who gently encourage, support, give freedom, and assist you at the right time and in the right place.

What You Should Know about Grief that Heals

I want to take a moment to introduce a few basic facts about the grief response that will help you deal with your loss. Keeping in mind that your learning is an ongoing process, what follows is one of many beginnings.

- Grief is your response to deep love—an essential of life. Whenever you choose to love, as we all do, you automatically choose to grieve. It's a given, the other side of the coin of love. So look at your grief as something that anyone should expect following the death of a loved one. It feels horrible, but it is an expected human response to universal loss and change. It always works naturally and with precision, if you get out of the way and allow it to flow. In short, grief is good; it's the road of light through the darkness.

- Grief is not merely universal—it is exclusively individual. It can be strong or weak, brief or prolonged, immediate or delayed, distorted or erratic. Everyone grieves in their own style. Forget about so-called stages you are supposed to go through; they really only exist in theory. There is nothing wrong with you because you feel so sad, hopeless, despaired, fearful, angry, and alone. Or that you cry constantly, or can't cry at all—and yet someone else deeply affected by the loss is responding differently. The upside is, it does get better. You will survive and grow; that is the factual history of loss. It has been proven over and over again.

- Emotional wounds heal if we don't keep them raw and flowing by refusing to release them. Try giving yourself permission to heal and gradually let go of repetitive, hurtful thoughts. Yes, your sadness is deep and real, and you believe it will never end. Yet you must not use it as reason to shun reinvesting in life. Force yourself to do what you dislike doing by allowing the pain to flow out of you. That is what leads to healing.

- There is such a condition as legitimate suffering. It is inevitable, an innate part of the human condition, and comes from the unavoidable changes of life. Life is hard, and suffering is part of the package. No one is happy all the time. So go with the present conditions of life and try not to fight them.

- As you mourn, it is critical to remember that your past does not determine your future, unless you allow it to. Letting go of such a belief is the beginning of reinvesting in life. Grief is not only a necessary, ongoing process, a release, and repositioning—but it causes us to pause and learn. Be open to the new and unfamiliar. Be open to mystery and the unexpected. There is no greater challenge in grieving than to let the grief process play out.

- What we really do in the mourning process is to start a transition, in effect to build a new persona and way of life. You work toward a different normal, an unusual normal, a new normal, and at first no one likes it. Sometimes the identity changes are subtle; sometimes they stick out like a sore thumb. Yet they are a positive part of adapting to change, embracing the unfamiliar.

- Healing grief is a natural process; the emphasis is on *natural*, although healing can feel foreign and without merit. This means you can't rush it along in any way or push it aside; from out of nowhere, it will pop back up in discouraging ways. Healing is highly influenced by expectations of or resistance to the process. Its results are measured in a shift in the way we see the world and the way we live.

- We can choose to learn to love in separation. As I said earlier, you grieve because you loved well. Flourish from the experience of loss by learning to continue to love, albeit in separation. You can keep your loved one's memory alive in your heart forever, celebrate the life lived at appropriate times, and continue on in the next chapter of your life. Believe, as many therapists and mourners do, that healing is essentially a spiritual journey, since spiritual crises are common when we are overwhelmed by events that don't fit our view of the world.

What Healing Is Not

As you can well imagine, healing does not mean that once you feel you have finished actively grieving and have accepted your loss, you will be like your old self once again. Anyone who suffers the loss of a loved one never truly returns to their previous life and becomes their old self again. Why? Because all of those interactions with the deceased loved one cannot be reproduced, and life will always be different from the way it was. Different does not mean, though, that life will be worse than the way it was before. Life could also be different for the better. It all depends on you.

The best way to consider healing is that it is a continuous, ongoing event—a lifelong growth experience. Growth is all about living life in a better way. That is why healing is in many ways a higher calling: we take new roads, do new things, make new sacrifices, and mature in the process. It is a journey of self-discovery. As we heal, just like a broken bone, we get stronger and discover a new inner strength. And when grief revisits, as it surely will, our present condition of healing can be used to manage the hurt in a different way.

We can use the lessons learned to minimize the hurt, accept the reminders of our loss as normal, and gently let them go just as they come into our thoughts. These lessons come from several sources: friends, family, readings, others who have coped well, unexpected happenings, and our spirituality. While one source may be most helpful, input from several sources is a common pattern.

Healing is not a cure. A cure implies an end. Healing proceeds and proceeds as it prepares us for the next chapter in our life. There is no end to the healing that we continually need. Healing is promoted by sharing grief and finding new ways to deal with the new conditions of life.

The Major Goal of Healing

What does it mean to successfully heal from suffering the death of a loved one? The operational answer is *peace of mind through radical acceptance*. The intent is to proceed with adapting and make choices with inner peace as your major consideration. Nothing beats a quiet mind for promoting growth and creativity. But it is also essential that you overcome inertia, and only you are responsible for doing that.

If you come from a peace-driven place within, you will be able to deal with grief when it revisits (as it surely will) and with the additional changes that have to be made. Such peace will have effects not merely on your inner life—it will revitalize your physiology as well. Refuse to depend on external circumstances alone for joy and meaning in life; highly value and continually focus on the control you have of your inner self.

One thing you can do immediately to help yourself experience inner peace is increase your ability to relate to others with courtesy, respect, and humility, even as you grieve. By making an effort to relate to others this way, you'll find yourself making repeated value-driven choices to reach this reachable goal. Repetitive positive decision-making will result in feeling better about yourself, reducing fear, and establishing routines that bring comfort. Forming these intentions is frequently an unused road to reinvesting in life and expanding beyond our boundaries.

Try asking the following question every day: what must I do differently to reduce the pain and manage my sadness? The key word is "differently." Notice this is an internally focused question asking what you can do, not what others should or can do. Become aware of the thoughts and circumstances that lead up to increased pain. What is the cascading first thought?

Perhaps you need to free yourself from what is frequently the scourge of many mourners: obsessive thinking. This act of changing past conditioning by itself will be a huge step toward peace of mind. Determine where you can short-circuit the behavior and thoughts that increase anxiety levels before they get out of control.

We cannot always avoid anxiety, but we can reality-test (determine fact from fiction) the fears, guilt, and anger that fuel it. Make a detailed examination of the truth or falsity of the thinking behind your emotions. Then make your choice to overrule inaccurate analyses. Self-healing demands this choice, since often these volatile emotions have little basis in reality. (See **#15, Silence Your Rude and Frightening Inner Voice**, in chapter 4.)

The first step to take at some point in your mourning is to decide that you want to diminish the pain and misery you are feeling. I cannot tell you when that will occur; only you can make the call. In short, you form the intention of reinvesting in life despite all of the feelings inside that say "no way." You may not be able to do it today, but you can work on it a little at a time.

Act as You Wish to Be

One of the secrets of human behavior is to discover that you can act your way into new beliefs, feelings, and assumptions about life. Yes, act. In doing so, you will break old thought-habits of dealing with adversities that aren't working. More importantly, you can pretend your way into feeling better and out of a negative mood. Simply begin with a strong commitment to try the new. Let nothing deter you.

One of the oldest self-help groups in the world, Alcoholics Anonymous, has a slogan that says, "Fake it 'til you make it." It works. This transformation—in essence an identity-shift—happens in someone's life every day. What they never thought could happen, within or without, suddenly emerges, due to their persistent make-believe behavior.

Act as you wish to be is an age-old recipe for adapting to change. Mere opinion? No. The world is full of people who started a task with great reluctance and came through with a new lease on life. Hard work? Yes. Yet it always works, if you do one thing: keep acting "as if."

This means acting as if you are where you want to be in your healing—until you actually get there. It has now become a habit. You break the unconscious patterns of thinking and feeling that are causing excessive suffering by staying aware of where you are in dealing with your loss. Actions often reflect unconscious thoughts and can be important clues for change. Carefully watch what you do and possibly keep a diary of your daily thoughts.

THE PROCESS OF HEALING

1. Get off of cruise control and become aware of your automatic negative judgments.

2. Observe what is happening within and compare it with your behavior. Conscious awareness of thoughts and accompanying behavior will be the key to molding positive coping responses.

3. Accept what you find, *especially your emotions*, and don't rationalize them. They are normal human responses, given the existing circumstances. Intervene with rational alternatives and start acting "as if" you are already at the point where you want to be.

4. Choose to anchor attention and "as if" behavior elsewhere. This is a powerful response. Here is the key understanding: healing requires both inner and outer changes.

5. Repeat positive actions to help erase the unconscious negative beliefs that you can't cope or are not good enough. These beliefs prolong healing. Repetition is essential. You will discover the power you have within. Try it and see for yourself. You will break the old patterns.

Let the following principles guide your grief work.

• Your unconscious mind, your database, is always open to positive or negative suggestions and will respond to them right away. It doesn't decide if what you say is good or bad; it runs with and tries to bring to fruition whatever you consciously say and do. Feed it with positive repetition to counter earlier programming. Keep affirming and acting "as if."

- Seek the wisdom of courageous role models (your heroes) and those who have coped well. I am reminded of Sir Isaac Newton's keen observation: "If I have seen further, it is by standing on the shoulders of giants." (See **#34, Utilize Quotations in Your Healing Process**.)

- Allow grief to run its natural course through you; don't block a natural process. This means willingly feel and face the pain; it will subside, reappear, and cycle again and again. That is to be expected. You are not weak.

- Practice forgiveness and humility—the gifts you give to yourself and the other person. Become more loving in all that you do, and you are guaranteed to find peace of mind. These actions never fail to deliver.

TWO

Five Gifts that Will Get You through Any Loss

Tell me and I'll forget; show me and I may remember; involve me and I'll understand.

—CHINESE PROVERB

Does the grief you are experiencing seem unreal? Are you expecting your loved one at any minute to come walking through the door? Do you feel that your life has come to an end without him or her? Are you are at a bottomless abyss, feeling out of control? Have you lost trust in your ability to continue on? These feelings and more are not unusual for many mourners. They are common characteristics of the sudden confrontation with change after the death of a loved one.

You seem to be losing your sanity; it just doesn't make sense. All of this is compounded by a series of obstacles: sudden feelings of abandonment, inability to find a good listener, lack of confidence to deal with the future, and lack of reliable information to help ease the searing pain of loss.

There is good reason for this. At root, self-education about coping with loss is nearly nonexistent—until a major loss occurs.

Then the search is on at a time when the disorganization and stress of grief is high.

However, it is never too late to begin the task of discovering the wide range of normalcy among grief reactions. Your style is just that, a unique response, be it healthy or unhealthy. And it may change as you progress. Despite your deep hurt, you will learn to confront your emotions and find that precious peace of mind. So refuse to give yourself a time limit within which to feel better.

Where can you start on this journey? As the Chinese proverb suggests, you must become involved to understand, to become motivated to manage change.

Five Gifts You Can Access with a Little Effort

A gift is not a reward; it is a sign of love. These five gifts of love are there for you to get through any confrontation with loss. They have been used by millions to deal with the new experiences that the death of a loved one forces all of us to face. Give them to yourself.

Gift 1. Knowledge about Grief and Grief Work

What is your purpose for reading this book? What are you hoping to find? Give it much thought, as it will provide insight into your most critical needs.

The unanswered questions about life and death are many, but the knowledge about what you are experiencing and how to deal with it exists; it's out there and has been used successfully again and again. No matter what your loss is like inside, there is something specific—just for you—waiting to be discovered.

The first place to begin your search for what is necessary for survival and adaptation is by considering friends and relatives who have suffered similar losses. Ask how they have coped with them (even ask people you don't know well). It is perfectly normal and smart to humbly seek out the wisdom of others who have been through similar losses. Yes, this is a tough time to have to go asking. However, finding resources is the mark of those who successfully manage the massive changes life continually presents.

The best suggestion I have is to consistently ask a simple question of others at an appropriate time: "What was the most helpful thing that got you though your loss?" You will obtain a variety of answers—some good, some not so good. Take their counsel seriously. Discard it, if you don't think it's right for you. Question professionals you may know; their input is valuable and may or may not be right for your circumstances. Also, be sure to search out your local community resources, such as churches, agencies, and hospital and hospice bereavement programs, and tap into them.

And remember, it *is* all right to ask why. Why did this have to happen?

MODELING: AN EFFECTIVE
COPING TECHNIQUE

Reach out for new knowledge. Don't allow pride or old cultural stereotypes to hold you back. Asking for help is an incredibly healthy and intelligent way to cope. There is so much experience out there of which you are not aware. Modeling another person's coping success will significantly reduce your unnecessary suffering. This is another reason to join a support group and/or bond with those who are filled with hope.

Find out what beliefs motivate them. Next, weigh benefits and disadvantages of their responses. Then decide if you want to use what you have heard or let it go as not applicable to your situation and goals. But remember, these people have gone through this experience and can share important details on what not to do, which can save you much energy and conflict.

Get all the specifics, all the theoretical and practical insights that are out there so you can jettison the myths. Also ask others who have been caregivers, the bereavement coordinator at your local hospice, or your local librarian to recommend readings on grief to support your quest to grow as you travel down this road. Don't settle for merely getting by; grow from the experience of loss.

Try searching the Internet, always considering the source, credibility, and generalizability of the information.

There are many helpful websites that have chat rooms where you can ask questions of others who are further along in their grief than you are. One contact may turn out to be the major source you need. Do a Google search on grief and you will find numerous choices. Consider starting or joining a reading group of others who are adapting to the death of a loved one, where you can discuss strategies that seem to work or not work. We can learn much and be motivated by each other. I hear this positive outcome all the time from members in grief support groups.

Prepare yourself for the stressful months ahead by reading everything you can on coping with massive changes. Examine the suggested readings list at the back of this book. Search the grief literature for some of the many quality resources available. Pamphlets, books, and articles on grief are abundant. You may not feel like reading anything early in your grieving process. If so, come back to this resource later. There is so much information from reading alone that can help you. Again, pick and choose what rings true for you, and discard the rest.

Gift 2. The Desire to Make Wise Choices

Desire, one of the most powerful forces in the universe, is never given its proper due. Desire fuels choice, the framework for who we are, and the quality of our coping ability. Everyone possesses the gift of choice, and we *always* have a choice about how we relate to our great loss and to ourselves.

Learning from and living with the loss of your loved one is directly dependent on what you choose. Wanting to adapt and making wise choices, especially the one you make regarding the *attitude to take into each day*, are crucial. Attitude is everything, especially the attitude you develop toward yourself.

Through the work of Dr. Martin Seligman, prolific author and authority on optimism and pessimism, we can clearly state that attitude is a better predictor of success in any endeavor, better than education, experience, or IQ. A good attitude is better for your health, your relationships, and the way you deal with the pain of loss. No matter how many losses you have had to face or the difficult years you have had to endure, *anyone* can choose to use the greatest motivator of all: the attitude of wise choosing—the attitude to keep on keeping on.

You are free to use practical wisdom to create the way you want to cope with the death of your loved one. You already have it within yourself, but you can add to it through learning before making a decision. My job in writing is to provide you with many alternatives; your job is to use your inner wisdom to choose with prudence and in accordance with your values. That wisdom is your master virtue; it defines you and your character.

Smart choice-making not only dictates how you cope with your great loss—it dictates the quality of your life and ultimately your health. The reduction of pain and the successful coping with the loss of your loved one are the sum total of what you decide to endure. Silently keep repeating these seven words over and over again: "I am free to choose my path." Then begin to examine each alternative. Suggestion and imagination are proven major players for creating choices and are indispensable for successful coping. Positive choices invariably bring positive results. The thought behind choice is where all healing begins.

You always have a choice about what you will do with how you feel at a particular time. Feelings don't own you; you own them. *Choose love. Choose possibility. Choose inner peace. Choose friends. Choose beauty.* By getting into the habit of embracing these opportunities, you begin to build the foundation for awakening new meaning. In turn, your choices feed the transformation that grief always demands. The result often brings you face to face with your spiritual identity and beliefs, closer to your higher power (God, Allah, etc.) and to your loved one. All of these can be powerful assets on the journey with loss. On the other hand, you may experience a spiritual crisis, wonder where God is when you need Him, and question your beliefs. Still, the above choices will play a special role in dealing with such a crisis.

One thing is sure: *coping with the death of your loved one presents numerous options and choices*, and they will play the pivotal role in finding peace and inner strength. It is a major part of your grief work to generate and discover options and then weigh the outcomes, pro and con, of the straightforward choices you have before you. Especially consider the outcome of not making the tough choice. Often a key question to be addressed is: what kind of a person do I want to be?

All of this suggests that when you are grieving, wisdom is about deciding to tap into the wealth of knowledge available and becoming aware of what you don't know. Allow your intuition, your innate wisdom, to play a role in decision-making; it will not lie or distort the truth. Trust your instincts, your gut, and your hunches. Your inner wisdom is in your whole body, not just the brain.

You possess and control the great freedom of choice to move toward the light of day. You *always* have a choice, and within lies a wise soul who can help you make the right one. If you seldom use your intuition, try to learn about this gift and how it can assist in coping with loss (see **#6, Trust Your Gut**).

Gift 3. Learning the Truth about the Death, and the Fact that Life Must Change

The third gift is a twofold truth. First, learning all of the details of how your loved one died, including the hour and day and the care received before the death, is essential. Not knowing will gnaw at you and cause unwanted anxiety again and again. Once you've discovered all the possible information, peace of mind will begin to set in.

Finding freedom for you may mean having to ask doctors or nurses, friends or relatives, strangers who were there, or some-one at the workplace what happened. Write letters, email, tweet, text, and make phone calls until all sources are exhausted. Then decide to live with what you know, as well as what you may never be able to know, about the death. I still do not know the exact cause of my child's death, and sometimes we have to live with that.

At the same time, you will also have to deal with the second inescapable truth: death transforms us, and we have to go with the changes. There is no option here. That is another reason why I mentioned in First Words that you will have to establish a new identity, a new you. The world is clearly a different place without your loved one. Therefore, to cope with new circumstances we have to do things we haven't done previously. "When we are no longer able to change a situation," said the famous psychiatrist and Holocaust survivor Viktor Frankl, "we are challenged to change ourselves." This applies to mourners and nonmourners alike. Learning about your new world only occurs in the present, and you are the only person who creates your own reality by what you think.

This implies having to adaptively change to meet the circumstances that are now part of life, whether you like them or not. That is a scary major challenge all people are destined to face. It means letting go of some of the habitual thought-patterns of the past or the way you used to deal with problems. But letting go means you are in charge and moving in a new direction. The good news is—even though you may not believe it at this time—you do have the inner resources to integrate your great loss into a new life.

Gift 4. Myth-Breaking

What do beliefs and myth-breaking have to do with coping well?

Everything! Everyone lives by some myths. But grief myths are among the most destructive. Myths that impede the grief process are false beliefs in hiding that create more suffering. Often we unwittingly become victims of our own beliefs. Developing awareness of damaging myths built on falsehoods, and discarding them, will help significantly in normalizing your grieving style and reducing conflict. Remember, all beliefs about death and grief have a powerful effect on behavior. Robert Hahn of the U.S. Centers for Disease Control and Prevention in Atlanta, Georgia, said, "Beliefs and expectations are not only conscious, logical phenomena, they also have physical consequences." This observation is especially important in terms of the grief process, specifically in losing strength and stamina, and eventually becoming ill.

Once you recognize the deep-seated beliefs that affect how you cope with loss, you will be able to release and replace those that are hindering progress. Since all behavior is habitual, there is nothing wrong with unloading unworkable beliefs and the myths they spawn, resulting in unwanted suffering. This is a critical choice you make. Your myths will play out in the way you lengthen or shorten your intense grief period. This is why finding credible grief resources is a must in order to dispel false information, negative thought-patterns, and half-truths. Myth-breaking is a key coping response.

COMMON MYTHS

There is an old Chinese proverb that says, "A child's life is like a piece of paper on which every person leaves a mark." Some of those marks are damaging to us. Become aware of some of the grief myths that have been instilled in you by the media or authority figures when you were young. These fables will have a major effect on how you feel about yourself (your self-image) and your behavior as you deal with loss. Here are a number of the most common ones:

▸ You should be over grief in a few weeks. *(Grief is not time-bound; the only time frame is the one you give it.)*

▸ Crying is a sign of weakness. *(Crying is a normal human response, not a male or female response.)*

▸ Grief only affects your emotions. *(Grief affects all aspects of the entire person.)*

▸ Grief means that eventually you are supposed to let go of the person who died. *(We don't let go. We love in separation in our own ways.)*

▸ You will be your old self again. *(We will not become our old selves again; our identities change and we grow.)*

▸ It is best to turn away from grief instead of toward it. *(Facing pain, not running from it, is part of grief work.)*

- There is a predictable and orderly stage-like progression for grieving. *(Grief unfolds in highly individual ways.)*
- The goal of grieving is to "get over" your grief. *(We don't get over it; we work toward relating to it differently.)*
- Grief and mourning are the same experience. *(Grief is the internal experience; mourning is the outward healthy expression.)*
- You shouldn't feel that way. *(Feelings just are. Accept where you are.)*
- Everyone needs to openly express every feeling. *(Some feelings are not hurtful if not expressed. It depends on individual needs.)*
- "Going to pieces" is abnormal grief. *("Going to pieces" is simply one way of expressing our grief.)*

The Most Damaging Myth

The myth with the longest-lasting and most hurtful consequences is this: you must let go of and sever ties to the deceased, find closure, and get on with your life. Closure usually implies closing the door of memories and the relationship. Not possible. True closure really means (1) accepting the absence of your loved one's physical presence, (2) releasing willful suffering, and (3) letting go of your old life while accepting the new one and a different relationship with the deceased.

Adherents to the monster myth of "letting go" have

usually been heavily influenced by those in the mourner's support system; these caregivers have grown tired of the ongoing pain and repetition of the grief process and want you to "get on with your life."

Myths, and the thoughts that accompany them, spawn added emotion, then questionable action or inaction, and finally results that bring more pain. Keep in mind this old Turkish proverb: "No matter how far you have gone on a wrong road, turn back." This applies to the myths about grief that you have been taught or are presently living by. Self-limiting myths and beliefs are especially damaging. This will be addressed in the next chapter.

Gift 5. Persistence

The final gift that will get you through any loss is summed up by Johann Wolfgang von Goethe, Germany's gifted man of letters: "Nothing in this world can take the place of persistence." Persistence is behind all great discoveries, overcoming difficulties, and making worthwhile changes in life. There is no escaping its necessity when grieving and having to break out of old habit patterns.

Initially, nothing can be more helpful than your conviction that you can eventually work your way through and adapt to the new circumstances of your life—to keep on persevering. Calvin Coolidge, the 30th U.S. president, said it best: "The slogan 'press on' has solved and always will solve the problems of the human race." Perhaps that is a reminder you might wish to put in a place where you will see it daily.

The will to persist transforms us and plays a pivotal role in all grief work. It is a significant trait in emotional resilience that you can develop regardless of past experiences. Persistence lies in the intent to do the new and the distasteful for as long as it takes. You simply have to practice and fail, practice and fail, and continue to outlast the disappointments, loneliness, fear, and pain. And you will. To fail is to learn. Repeat and repeat inside, "I am making it through this," even if you don't believe it at this time. Always say it in the present tense. You are your own best coach; change the wording so that it is more believable for you.

Once you embrace this adaptive mode of thinking (keeping on), you will be amazed at how the conditions of your life will gradually change for the better. Basically, you must want to reinvest in life despite the great void you face. What you believe becomes the reality you grieve in every day.

Check your limiting expectations about yourself, your ability to cope, and insist that you are capable of pressing on. Seek help in making this critical change, from a professional if necessary. Recognizing the power of positive expectation is the next step in persistence. And most importantly, remember that you possess the free will to change any expectation that destroys persistence.

Why is checking your limiting expectations so important?

Because we change behavior by changing expectations, not by motivation alone. What we expect and believe is who we are and how we talk to ourselves. Many unworkable beliefs ingrained in us early in life by well-meaning adults—through their example and comments—become the reality of our adult lives. Our behavior is dictated by conscious and strong unconscious beliefs that we hardly ever address.

However, they become deeply rooted within as "the truth" and prove to be especially devastating when they are negatively tied into how we should grieve the death of a loved one. Regrettably, adult grief models are notoriously unrealistic. The chances are high that you have some common misconceptions that are grounded in half-truths and popular beliefs, what Dr. Wayne Dyer, calls brain viruses, perpetuated by well-meaning adults.

A Crucial Task of Grieving: Establish New Routines

Like the ocean waves that continually wash up on the shoreline, keep at the task of establishing new routines, of living without the physical presence of your loved one. New habits of thinking and acting are part of the work of adaptation. When you falter on occasion, pick yourself up, re-evaluate, and go back into the fray. Don't exaggerate your mistakes. You will reach your goal. Inside you, inherently, you know what you have to do. Trust your inner voice of love, not the critical rude one. The right answers will show up when you need them. Then muster the courage to do the work suggested.

As you read the coping strategies in the pages ahead (in essence, these are all acts of persistence), there will be recommendations you cannot agree with at this reading. Come back to them later, when you are at a different level of grieving and at a different place in your head. What doesn't make sense now will be useful at another time as you relate to your loss differently over the coming months. That is the part of persistence that pays off.

In summary, you already have what you need to get started. Trust yourself. You are greater than you believe right now. The gifts of knowledge, choice, truth, myth-breaking, and persistence will be guides.

THREE

The Critical Overlooked Factor: Resilience

*Do you want to know who you are? Don't ask. Act!
Action will delineate and define you.*

—THOMAS JEFFERSON

Some mourners linger for months, even years, in the hopelessness of their grief. But others are able to integrate their great loss into their lives. Why? Although much has to do with early childhood maps of grief and death drawn by parents or other authority figures, there is another key factor: emotional resilience.

Being resilient means being willing to bounce back when you've taken a terrible life blow. Here's how bereaved mother Linda Murillo is doing it:

> "Without a doubt, [the emotionally resilient mourner] is the person who doesn't believe they can go down, that they must keep looking for the signs, seeing the gift, looking for the lesson. What have I learned and to whom have I given? That is the question I try to ask myself every day about my son's death."

Notice the other-centered focus on whom she has helped, what she has learned, and the action thoughts in Linda's statement, even though in pain. Emotional resilience is dealing with all of the "negative" emotions (they are really not negative, since all emotions have an adaptive function) that engulf you and not allowing them to take away your power. Although you may not think well of your ability to cope, you can still override past conditioning, choose to "see the gift" and "look for the lesson," adopt optimism over pessimism, and learn through trial and error. These are all part of emotional resilience. This means no excuses, which only promote the victimization attitude.

Ask any expert on coping with loss and you will be told that the mental approach you assume toward meeting this great change in your life is the backbone of emotional resilience. Old assumptions and ways of doing things have to go, or you'll never reach the ultimate goal of being able to accept what has happened. All too frequently, what we were once told or assumptions we may have had turn out not to be the way the world or grief works, and we have to alter our perceptions. For example, a common belief is that grief is an event, which implies a beginning and an end. Therefore, within a year at most you should be all better. Or we are told there is one right way to grieve, when in fact there are a multiplicity of right ways, depending on the individual and his or her perception of death.

Perceptions are the personal meaning we give to experience. We can all have a similar experience, but we usually perceive it differently. And, we change our perceptions by changing behavior and the way we think about the world. These changes occur from experience, as does learning that death is part of life and gives great meaning to it. Altering mental patterns is an important step and a major factor in happiness, sadness, or overcoming fear. If you hang on to old patterns of dealing with loss, you cannot expect to cope well with perpetual change.

So how do we counter misinformation at a time like this? Let me explain.

The Most Important Coping Response You Can Develop

Why do some mourners find useful information about coping with loss, eliminate unnecessary suffering, and look forward? The answer is daily action, the core of resilience, the forgotten factor. No action, no change. Action dispels fear. Outward change forces inner change. *You must take daily action toward acceptance and reinvesting in life.* Although painful at first, actions—both within and without—then become useful habits.

When should you start? Only you hold the answer. Here is what thirty-eight-year-old Kathleen, a psychiatric nurse practitioner, told me she did:

> I find it a bit difficult to point to one particular thing that helps me cope with the death of my mom, as I tend to believe that it's a combination of things that helps me survive the worst loss of my life so far. However,

I will say that my faith in God and daily prayer, combined with memories/photos of my mom, have been helpful as I make my personal journey through grief. Of course, my deep faith coupled with prayer comes from my mom, so that's an added comfort, since I see this as a gift my mom gave to her children.

Other beneficial tools, behaviors, etc., in no particular order: working on the program for my mom's memorial mass with my sister and planning the reception; a grief support group; allowing myself to weep and feel sad sixteen months later; talking about my feelings to understanding friends; walking as much as possible; reading novels that have characters who have experienced significant loss (I'm getting back to borrowing books from the library); sharing memories and feelings with my sister Maryann and brother Joe; relying on what I learned from my professional training, for example, D. W. Winnicott's writings on "the capacity to be alone," John Bowlby's *Attachment and Loss* trilogy, and Judith Viorst's *Necessary Losses*. Gardening/growing plants and flowers and being outdoors in the sun helps!

It's helpful to talk to people who "get it," as they tend to be folks who have survived their own terrible losses. When I'm up for it, I think creating a memorial project will foster another dimension of healing. Specifically, I have hundreds of letters and cards from my mom that I've kept over the years. It's still too painful for me to organize them, but I was able to hold a bunch of them close to my heart a couple of weeks ago, prompting a flood of tears. I'd like to write a poem or series of poems tentatively titled "Legacy of Letters." When I find myself getting too close to the "abyss," I remind myself that my mother enjoyed her life and was an upbeat person. I know she would want me to cultivate happiness as much as possible and really *live* the balance of my life on earth.

It is not hard to lose our spirituality and become externally referenced, losing touch with our deep inner selves. Try applying what you learn in the pages ahead with creating a specific designed behavior. Don't wait until you feel like it before you act. *It is essential to understand that behavior changes attitudes and feelings.* You can behave differently, even if you feel it isn't going to help at the present moment.

Embrace the following as a strong belief: it's not what you did yesterday, it's what you do today that counts. Try not to dwell on what you should have done. Vowing to take a positive action toward resolving your pain and suffering is at the center of adapting to change; it will eventually change your feelings, which tend to dominate decision-making. Try something, anything, as opposed to staying in your bubble, like writing down one thing daily that you want to accomplish.

Learning does little good unless you do something with it. You will hear me say "take action" frequently in your reading.

Underline it each time you read it and decide when you will put what you learn into the form of a specific behavior on that particular day.

So what other forms might action take? Here are four essential starters.

Tell Yourself that You Will Get through This

We talk to ourselves all the time (often without full awareness), and what we say each moment lays the groundwork for how we cope with our great losses. What you're going through is a terrible, soul-wrenching experience, but if you remind yourself on a daily and consistent basis that you will get through it, you'll plot a course for continued grief healing.

Become aware of and change your inner monologue when necessary. Reject what puts you in a downward spiral; this means creating new thoughts.

Repeat and repeat in your self-talk that healing is doable—this begins the journey to acceptance in your heart and is, where it really counts.

If you do not believe what you are telling yourself, then begin immediately to examine those feelings and their underpinning attitude. Where did they come from and how can they be challenged? We are what we believe. Change them and you will make strides in enhancing the quality of your ability to cope well.

Your constant self-suggestions are another powerful force leading to the creation of new beliefs. So too are the suggestions of others, which is why you will need to examine them carefully. Ultimately, suggestions and their corresponding actions become an integral part of transformation. Transformation means change in behavior, outlook on life, spirituality, interests, and patience.

Begin by changing the negative language you use about getting through your loss. Keep asking your unconscious mind, "What do I need to cope with this loss?" and it will give you answers that will help in the journey. The wisdom is within, waiting to be tapped; everyone possesses it. Will you listen to it?

Be your own best coach and talk within about things that are uplifting, anything that gives a hint of inspiration. Don't talk trash to yourself; be gentle and loving. Let's face it. That's not easy to do when you are down. This is where courage—and you have it—must kick in. It is there to perform, if you call on it, as those before you have demonstrated.

Engineer Small Successes

Although absolutely essential, positive self-talk alone is not a cure-all. Let's be real—changing thoughts without following though by doing will have limited effects. You must start engineering small successes in order to realize you can make it through this major life change. Without question, repetitive positive action will elevate self-esteem and is a key coping factor. Make a plan to get yourself through this particular day (even the next hour) or one that you believe will be most difficult for you. Be specific in who you will be with and what you will do. Then make the hard decision and follow it.

Maybe finding a part-time job or volunteering would be a success for you. Getting through your tax return by yourself for the first time could be another. When eating, concentrate all of your attention on the food, and let go of your sad thoughts for a short time. Eating certain foods with friends and family can be highly relaxing and symbolic. See how long you can give yourself some downtime so you can reenergize. There is nothing wrong in treating yourself well while you mourn; one helps the other.

Find something to take on and go for it, as that success will strengthen your inner life. As you achieve and find additional successes, joy will slowly return to thoughts of investing in life and the way you perceive your great loss.

Celebrate the Small Stuff

Recognize how far you have come. When you review your day, credit yourself for where you are in your grief work. Every hour, every day is a victory. Give yourself a pat on the back for small victories, even if they don't feel like victories. Constantly remind yourself of the successes of the past in dealing with your grief, your work, or in any aspect of your life. When you talk to yourself, give compliments: *"I am kind, loving, and strong. I am coping. I am gaining."* If it has only been a month, even several months since your loss, note that you are still going.

Every day, tell yourself you will keep at it and know that your new routines will eventually bring change for the better. Your consistent action to adapt will make the difference. Savor the process of progress. Celebrate that progress with a friend you trust and who knows your pain.

Start and End Each Day with Gratitude Memories

But wait a minute, you say. You want me to show gratitude, feeling the way I do? Yes! It is not easy to give thanks when shrouded in the pain of loss. But gratitude is the energy force that will punch a hole in your pain and bring stress relief. It will be especially useful when you feel that downward spiral, and anxiety over your loss builds.

Gratitude is one of the mental processes that makes a huge difference in strengthening our inner life. It reduces thoughts of limitation, creates a healthy perspective, and brings the realization that your loved one will always be a gift you were given.

Review each day for the good things that happened—an old friend called, you had great energy and a good night's sleep for a change, you got a raise in pay, your computer is working well, your friend brought over a great meal, etc.—and fully immerse yourself in the good feelings. This is sound mental health in the making. Like any other life-affirming attitude, gratitude has been shown to change physiology for the better. But set the tone by starting it early in the day.

Gratefulness will help you cope with your loss as you begin to appreciate all, seen and unseen, that is supporting your efforts.

An act of daily thanksgiving will add to the inner change you seek. Remember all of the little things we all take for granted—the ability to see, hear, touch, and create. Also, develop awareness of what cannot be taken from you. As one mourner said, "I'm grateful every day when I wake up." The gratitude mindset takes work, but it is life-affirming and helps immensely in leading to acceptance.

You should also review your life with the deceased, and pick out some life gratitude memories. Look back on all the good things those close to you did for you early in life. Focus on all that was given and again immerse yourself in the feeling of being loved by your loved one and a higher power. Begin a gratitude list and watch it grow each day. It will change the inner landscape of your life and bolster your faith as you begin to see the road ahead with new eyes. You will be surprised and appreciate what continues to be added to your world. (See chapter 6, **#88, Build a Data Bank of Gratitude Memories**.)

• • •

In the final analysis, a new mindset, action, and little successes will be the determining factors in eliminating unnecessary suffering and stress from your time of mourning.

I reemphasize, in the process of adapting, get rid of the notion that you can't have some moments of joy and inner peace. We all need them to balance the sadness, which is temporary and normal, and the accumulation of negative thoughts that constantly seep into our thinking. No one can continually stay immersed in the pain of loss without becoming ill; constant grieving is unsustainable. Hopeless deep grieving is disabling.

Putting your grief away for a short period of time is a *critical coping technique*.

All mourners need relief. It's okay to smile, accept an invitation to dinner, or have a laugh without feeling guilty—that's part of the *action* you can take, and another small (or sometimes large) success. It will prepare and recharge you to return to and continue adapting to your great loss. You will never lose the memories of your loved one by this necessary time out.

To summarize, utilizing the most important coping response for managing change, action, demands three things:

▸ Sustained effort, commitment, and willingness to stay with your plan.

▸ Consistent self-monitoring on the four essential starters. Accept taking a fall as not unusual. But get back up again and again, and never give up.

▸ Visualize—a powerful but little-used coping response— exactly what you want to accomplish each day before you tackle it. Picture it clearly, with all the details including the weather, taking it step by step. Believe you will make it if you take action on the how of your plan.

FOUR

Inner-Strength Healing Strategies

Everything can be taken away from a man but one thing: the last of human freedoms—to choose one's attitude in any given set of circumstances, to choose one's own way.

—Viktor Frankl in *Man's Search for Meaning*

The adversity you are now facing, as you begin to cope with the loss of a loved one, will reshape your inner life. It is inside, deep within, where you win the lifelong battle with change. You have all the tools there, and with your full commitment, they will be brought to bear at the proper time. Success in coping with your loss depends upon developing a clear this-is-what-I-want list and deciding you will not be dominated by the negative aspects of your loss (for example, "I should have done more," "I should have called another doctor," "No one knows what I'm going through"). That is self-torture.

Make up your mind that you will grow through your experience and learn more about yourself and life. By drawing on resources from within, this loss will ultimately forge in you a strong inner life that will prepare you for the changes yet to come.

By developing your inner life and the ability to persevere, you will emerge with greater awareness and new insights.

Where Will You Begin?

There is one proven way to change your attitude, which is behind all successful coping: change your thinking. Anyone can do it. You can make changes in your life if you do three things:

- Acknowledge that who you are is defined primarily by what you do and think.
- Believe you can change what you do and how you think over time.
- Never forget: attitude, your gateway to emotional resilience, is highly influenced by where you place your attention.

Once again, every day you have a choice about the attitude you will bring to your coping response; your attitude will either increase the intensity of grief and unnecessary suffering or work for you to overcome an obstacle as you feel the pain.

We turn now to remedies for coping with your loss and developing your inner life that have been used successfully by thousands of mourners. Decide what strategies you can begin to apply immediately. Success in coping with loss depends upon having a clear destination and deciding you will not be immobilized by the tasks that lie ahead.

1. Turn to, or Create, Your Nurturing Support Network

Follow your heart; it will lead you to the right people. We all need each other. It could be a parent, friend, sibling, other family, or a church group member—anyone who will listen, care, and support. Interdependence is a crucial commodity, and at a time of great loss it is always wise to seek assistance. Find someone who can help you deal with the reality of your powerlessness.

Educate your support system by gently telling them exactly what you need at a given time or what you feel you will need in the future: to be alone; to talk about what you are feeling at the moment; to say your loved one's name out loud; or to cry without them becoming upset. By all means, give your support system feedback. Be specific about how they are helping as well as what you need and when they should back off. Make every effort to do this in a gentle and sincere manner.

Although normally you know your needs better than anyone else, the early part of the grieving process can be a time of confusion. Mourners often "don't know what they don't know." This phrase implies that the awareness of what is normal and needed to mourn in a healthy way is commonly absent. Decide who you feel is best equipped to meet your immediate needs, be they emotional, legal, spiritual, financial, related to housing, or much greater. These are real needs, and your trusted support person(s) in the journey to managing loss can be there for you; they will help you reinvest in life. Find one person who believes in you, and this person will be a precious outlet for you during your time of grief.

Admittedly, this can be a difficult time to have to think about building such an important resource, if you have no one nearby to turn to. However, you can do a great deal in shaping your support network. The key understanding is nurturing—we all need it. You may have friends who want to help but don't know what to do. Give them little jobs: you will be helping them as they are helping you.

Be cognizant of the fact that some friends are better listeners than others. Consider finding a grief companion or hopefully companions. An old Chinese proverb states: "To know the road ahead, ask those who are coming back." One mother was able to talk to another mother who had also suffered through the death of her child. A widower was able to talk daily to another widower. And the person does not necessarily have to be someone who has recently suffered a great loss. Grief companions are arguably among the most valuable way to deal with loss; they stick by you. Knowing you are not alone in your struggles will make a world of difference.

Don't Resist Seeking Support

To communicate and relate is a major resource for coping well, but society does not accept mourners who need long-term support. Many mourners want it and need it, especially if they were overdependent on the loved one who died. It is not a sign of weakness to reach out for or accept help, even on a long-term basis. And yes, there are some people who do not need assistance, but few fall into this category. You will be introduced to a lot of high-quality information within an accepting atmosphere.

If you choose to seek support in a grief group, you can learn much from other mourners who are at different phases in their grieving and transformation. For example, often times, mourners do not realize that there are many secondary losses, in addition to the major loss, that they must acknowledge and openly grieve. Losses such as companionship, finances, sexual intimacy, and meaning, among others, are frequently significant secondary losses.

Remember that the fabric of social connections you have is unique just to you and no one else, and it becomes the biggest predictor of successful loss management. You will sense intuitively whom to speak to about your feelings and whom to ask advice from as the days go on. These individuals will help you meet a most critical need: to validate (to confirm) your great loss. Dialogue has been and always will be a great antidote for pain.

Historically, the American culture, influenced in the early days by Northern European tradition, has taught us to keep our feelings under guard, and the expression of tear-filled emotion is often still considered a sign of weakness. Add to this the fact that the emotions most commonly associated with grieving—anger, guilt, fear, and depression—have the tendency to isolate the mourner and keep some potential support people at a distance. All of this converges at a time when we need one of the most valuable coping techniques, social interaction to give us balance in our healing.

Most important of all, your support persons will provide hope in place of hopelessness and bring a sense of safety. Hope comes from the simple gift of human presence. Consider some of the positive steps you can take:

- If you are living alone, after relatives have left, a week or two after the death, invite a close friend or an adult child to stay overnight with you. This will provide not only a listener you need, but also a companion who can help reduce anxiety by presence alone. Seek this assistance depending on the availability of the support person and your needs to adjust to living by yourself.

- Listening fills a basic need to be heard and to feel we are understood and appreciated. If you choose to join a support group, consider befriending someone you intuitively feel would be a good listener and be there for the long haul. Good listeners mysteriously raise our energy levels. If you can find a grief companion who will also be an accountability partner, he/she can do much to reinforce your new routines and thoughts about your new life, developing your "new normal." This person can also act as a sounding board for your ideas on coping with loss as well as give an opinion if you seek one.

- Find someone who not only understands what you are feeling, but is available for you at all times of the day. Don't forget to use your telephone to call friends you know will listen, even if it's late at night.

- Do not be afraid to ask for help from professionals. The search for support obviously begins with close family members and friends, who may or may not be of great help. Yet there are many professional counselors, therapists, nurses, some clergy, and social workers who are experts in helping the bereaved and can ease your pain and suffering.

One of your major tasks of grieving is to strengthen your links to others, especially those who love life. Then you will be assured to learn from your loss as you keep the memory of your loved one alive in your heart.

2. Give Yourself Permission to Express Your Emotions

An old Turkish proverb states, "He that conceals his grief finds no remedy for it." Going public with grief is a critical action to take to reduce the physical stress and anxiety you may be feeling. Here is where your support network comes in to help. Explain what you are feeling to those you trust. Your number one self-healer will be sharing sensitive issues, negative and positive thoughts, and emotions freely. This is not a short-term process.

When you find safe places and safe people who verbally and nonverbally give you permission to express feelings without disguising them, not only will you feel better, you will be aiding the adjustment process. This process is the gradual acceptance of your new environment without the physical presence of your loved one. Having a shoulder to lean on is a normal human response; it helps you manage your inner life so that the process of accommodating change can be a major focus. A bonus of expressing emotions is that the immune system becomes more active, reducing the incidence of viral and bacterial infections common when mourning.

Acknowledge You Are Hurting

You may have to allow yourself the freedom to hurt. Admit that you are in pain—don't run from it. In fact, accepting it and feeling it is a big part of "good grief." Talk about whatever anger or guilt you may be harboring as well as if you think you might be depressed. (Keep in mind, though, that sadness and depression are often confused with one another.) These are all common, normal emotions related to grief that may or may not be a major part of your mourning process. They may be mixed with a host of negative emotions that must be aired and neutralized. Review your relationship and memories of your loved one, both the positive and those that were challenges, with your nurturing community as often as you feel necessary. If you don't, they will endlessly reappear, adding to your pain.

It is okay to repeat yourself. However, prepare yourself for some support persons who may not understand that repetition is an important part of healing and may be turned off by hearing you say something one day and repeat the story days later. This is not your problem; it's theirs, and you may have to say something about your need in this regard. Since we are built to vocalize and express feelings, make every effort to be open with feelings and describe what is happening within; it will reduce unnecessary physical suffering.

On the other hand, on some days you may not feel like talking about your feelings. If so, consider an alternative means of expression. It could be something in the expressive arts: drawing, music, movement, artwork, or writing (see **#70, Use the Expressive Arts**) or it could be something you do manually, like chopping wood or building or craftwork. Any of these are good substitutes and will provide relief even when you are able to freely express your emotions. As mentioned earlier, healing is an ongoing process, and various tools of expression, including vigorous activities, will facilitate the strengthening of your healing powers and reduce emotional pain.

3. Recognize When Denial Has Run Its Course

Denial is an unconscious defense mechanism that keeps something hurtful out of our conscious awareness. That is to say, it only works when you don't know you are using it. It often comes into play to numb the intense pain early in the grief process. Denial is not disbelief ("I can't believe he's gone"); it is actually a two-edged sword—useful at first in helping to ward off the full thrust of the loss. On the other hand, it prolongs the grief process when it causes the mourner to act as though the loved one has temporarily gone away and will eventually return.

Initially, it is a supportive defense since it gives us time to gradually assimilate the reality of the loss, the fact that the person has really died. At some point, however, we have to allow the unvarnished truth of what has happened to surface and face the pain. This is illustrated by a patient of mine who was grieving the death of her husband. She said that about eight months after his death she woke up one morning, reached her hand over to the other side of the bed—as she had been doing for months—to see if he was there. Again, no luck. She said, "It finally hit me. He is not going to be there again. Ever! I have to start doing something more to adapt and let go of old expectations." And she did, from that day on.

How long the denial of death lasts varies with the individual mourner. It could be hours, weeks, or months. Which leads me to a question you may be asking yourself right now…how can we know if we are in denial for too long?

The answer: carefully examine your behavior. It will give you clues to the unconscious beliefs you are harboring. We all have our times when we are not sure of what prompted our behavior. But studying that specific behavior is the key to uncovering the unconscious assumptions and beliefs behind it.

Denial, if present, will show up in what you do or refuse to do, as well as how you think. For example, are you thinking that your loved one will call or walk through the front door very soon? That he or she is away on a business trip? Do you look for him or her in certain places where you used to meet? Are you reminded of him or her in places you have to drive by, or do you intentionally go there to look for or find your loved one? Have you refused to do anything with his clothes because he may need them on his return? In contrast, ask yourself what specific things you are doing to actively adapt to and reinvest in life without the physical presence of your loved one.

The overuse of denial delays the inevitable, keeping you in a state of limbo. It then becomes necessary to create a pattern of thinking that acknowledges the loved one is not going to return and that you must start developing new routines and taking on new responsibilities accruing from the loss. In short, be a "proactive griever," take the initiative, and consciously make the adjustment to massive change happen. It begins by giving yourself a "why" to live.

4. Don't Miss an Opportunity to Cry

If you cry (not everyone does), be assured it is a natural way to cope with loss. Accept crying as a normal release, since it is a cleansing mechanism and not a sign of weakness, a way of showing love, not despair.

We cry for all sorts of reasons: when we are happy, sad, fearful, sympathetic, sometimes when we are angry, as well as when we are moved by a variety of events. Some people cry in church, mosques, and synagogues, especially when they go the first few times without their loved one. Others cry when they hear a special song that sparks a memory. I often cry when I see the families and friends of our young men and women who are killed in combat guarding our freedoms. This is probably related to the death of my daughter and the seeming waste of young lives. Crying is the most misunderstood coping tool we possess, whether mourning or not.

Crying has always been a natural human resource that has been misinterpreted in some cultures for centuries as something to be avoided. Give yourself the freedom to "let go" of your emotions since you will feel better and recharged, and continue on with your grief work.

But what if you can't cry, because you were brought up to believe you had to keep a "stiff upper lip"? Find another outlet, such as writing, drawing, or painting, talking out loud about your sadness, or exercising (see **#31, Find Physical Outlets for Emotional Stimuli: Exercise**). It's okay if you don't cry. Not everyone can. If you are concerned that you can't cry, perhaps a visit to a counselor to deal with previous unresolved losses or earlier recollections of abandonment might be considered. In any event, take action to allow inner feelings to surface, come out, and be recognized according to your needs in some manner.

5. When Panic Hits, Slow Down

Although many grievers find that they have times when their think-ing is slowed and confused, when panic strikes, thoughts seem to be rapid-fire. Finances, the children, where to live, where to find work, future companionship, how to find a way out of the torment—all these thoughts collide and bring out the possible fear-filled scenarios.

Make every effort, with professional help if need be, to discover the core issue that precipitates your panic; at root, it is all about fear. Fear is the rocket fuel for panic. Conquer fear and you conquer panic.

Robert Veninga, in *A Gift of Hope*, writes "You stop panic by reversing negative thoughts. You stop panic by ceasing to dwell on your fears or dreary prognoses or feelings that you can never again be happy or well." What do you put in their place? Just the opposite. Possibilities that are still yours, reasons to be committed, gratitude for the love you still have, and people who can help you through this difficult time. In short, you must begin to work on becoming an expert on changing your expectations and beliefs that you can control everything. Changing thought-patterns is a potent lifelong survival skill I have recommended for years (see **#67, Whatever You Focus On Increases in Size and Impact**).

PROVEN METHODS TO MINIMIZE PANIC ATTACKS

Finding what helps you is an individual trial-and-error experience. Next to sharing your fears and dealing with specific negative thoughts, panic attack therapy can also include the use of herbs such as passionflower, chamomile, linden flower, valerian, and lemon balm to help you relax. However, talking back to your negative thoughts is essential—at the first sign of fear. You can regain control of your thought processes by accepting, not maximizing, what is. One way to deal with a higher level of anxiety, before a full-blown panic attack sets in, is to practice your favorite relaxation technique. Relaxation techniques and exercise are a must. For example, make a slow deep-breathing exercise part of your initial response and focus all of your attention on the sound of your breath.

Certain foods are also culprits that heavily influence panic attacks. Analyze your diet for some of the foods associated with producing bodily stress as part of your self-therapy. Sugar is one of the biggest initiators, because it gives you a rush, but then a letdown. More importantly, it lowers blood sugar levels, which affect mood and behavior, often generating much anxiety.

Caffeine and alcohol are also contributors to anxiety, as are processed foods because they contain large quantities of preservatives. Too much caffeine depletes vitamin and mineral stores and removes water from the cells, adding to the lethargic feeling. If possible, eliminate it from your diet, as it can clearly contribute to panic.

Decide on an action you will take to challenge the thoughts and terrible physical feelings that are common with fear and high anxiety. The twin sibling of fear is worry, which may limit where you go and what you do in a vain attempt to avoid panic.

Love and make time for yourself every day—a warm bath, self-hypnosis, an active diversion, soft music. Meditation is also useful in reducing and controlling panic attacks.

If, for whatever reason, you are unable to make headway by yourself, get evaluated by your health care provider, who has experience with panic disorder and prescribing useful medication. You may also receive additional information by going to the Anxiety Disorders Association of America website at www.adaa.org.

6. Trust Your Gut

Although everyone possesses it, we seldom consciously use our intuitive nature as we grieve. Listen to what your intuition, dreams, and certain physical feelings—all ways the unconscious talks to the conscious mind—tell you about the choices to be made and the direction to travel. The body is a major resource of early warning information, so learn to consult your gut. If you feel it is right in your heart and soul, be assured, at that moment, you are right. Frankly, the suggestion may not be easy to do, but it will be right for you.

You have great wisdom within, if you will take the time to be honest with yourself and listen, so practice using your intuition and be open to creative flashes of insight. Ask questions and listen. Then make yourself take that first difficult step in tackling whatever problem you have to face that day.

TRY THIS EXERCISE

When discouraging thoughts start to build, take action to stop the downward spiral. Don't allow yourself to become frozen in self-doubt. Useful action is always preceded by recognizing that your emotional destiny is in your hands, if you want to successfully cope with your great loss.

Sit comfortably with legs uncrossed, close your eyes, and take a few deep breaths. Then ask yourself, "What do I need to do right now?" Be still and see what pops into your mind. What does it feel like?

Follow with, "What is the probable outcome of my choice versus my inaction?" Think in terms of desirable outcomes or, as many personal coaches say, "Start from the end." Again, recognize it may not be the easiest choice. And, on occasion, you may have to tolerate some inaction.

Listen carefully to what comes up from your intuitive treasure, and reverse the spiral. You may hear a voice, feel a tingling, have a vision, see an image, recall a memory, have an idea pop into your mind, or see something that reminds you of what needs to be done. Keep repeating the new action suggested.

Be patient, continue to ask, and listen to the wisdom within, which will lead you to a sense of well-being. However, be aware of the possibility of confusing wishful thinking and desires with your intuition. Rule both out. Ask yourself if either applies to what you receive, and couple that question with a prayer for making a wise choice, when information comes into your thoughts from the wisdom within. Then plan on how to implement the ideas in making choices and taking action.

With conscious use of your intuition, you can redirect emotion. You can access the wisdom of your authentic voice through serenity skills like meditation and the relaxation response, and connect more intimately with your spiritual intelligence. Again, be aware of what pops into your mind during meditation time. Could this information come from your beloved or a divine being? Many believe that God or the loved one works through intuition to make contact and give ideas. Coping well depends solely on how and what you think. We create the thoughts that create the emotions. Coping well, like finding meaning and purpose, which are essentially spiritual questions, is always inside of you. Listen!

To summarize: if you want to be transformed, trust your inner voice and your best intuitions, and become aware of your natural intuitive style. The wisdom we need is there for the asking and the listening. Stay in the moment. Western culture has trained us to dismiss this useful resource. Consult your heart first, and your reason will catch up later. Trust yourself to make the choices and decisions that present themselves. We all possess that inherent capability to profit. We are much more than we ever imagine.

7. Allow Grief to Revisit—Don't Fight It

Reencountering feelings of intense grief (and crying), especially in the early months of your loss, is normal. Sometimes called "grief attacks," these episodes are usually triggered unexpectedly. It could happen when watching a movie, seeing an intact family, hearing of a similar loss, smelling something, hearing a song, or having a sudden flashback to an old memory involving the deceased. It could be anything! It is okay to take an expression break by crying, talking, writing, or using another mode of emotional expression when you feel you need it. We all have a need for emotional release at this time. *It is a normal human response to have unexpected emotions resurface.* Accept painful reminders as a function of memory, not as an indicator that your progress is lacking.

Be especially kind to yourself when things have gone well for several days or weeks, and all of a sudden you have a major "grief attack" triggered by an unexpected event or a specific thought. You may read about the death of a stranger, or be at the grocery store and see a young couple shopping, and it strikes a deep chord within. Keep telling yourself that, even though you thought you were past this point in your grief, this is all normal, normal, normal.

Again, find someone to talk to about what is happening inside, and give yourself permission to let grief, with all of the emotion, go through you naturally. Sharing your pain and finding words of encouragement throughout the months and years is essential self-care, just as it was in the early days of your loss.

8. Cultivate a Bit of Solitude for Yourself

Take time out each day just for yourself. This is just as important as building your circle of interpersonal relationships. Find your own small space of contentment in the fury of the changes you are facing and feed your soul. Solitude is a positive-state leading to comfort, enhanced spirituality, and creative coping with your great loss. Plan for some time alone. Make a list of the things that you want to do with this alone time that will ease your suffering or that will help you relax. Use that list to nurture yourself at this time.

It is important to make sure you are comfortable with your surroundings in your solitude. Find a place where you enjoy being alone—a particular room in your home, in a church, an area in a park, at the beach, or some other natural setting. If you are afraid to be alone at this time in your grief, ask your most trusted friend to be with you. Ask the special person to take a quiet walk with you.

Solitude can balance the heavy stress you are under and raise your energy level; it is also an excellent opportunity to connect with your spiritual side and access the insight of your positive inner voice, so often overlooked when grieving. Here is the time to read something that will help you cope—daily inspirational verses or poetry.

Also, use solitude time to give yourself an additional pep talk. Do what is best for you. Allow this timeout to become one of your new lifelong routines, as it will become a major source of strength. It can generate renewed energy to enhance your ability to see additional possibilities and choices. Planning your solitude will take three or four weeks to become a daily habit. Sticking with it is worth the dividends it will bring to your inner life. In short, make silence a practice, and it will restore your interest in the world.

MAKE A RELAXATION SIGN

As part of your solitude time, take a few moments to practice using a relaxation sign that can be used anytime or anywhere you need to relax. For example, give yourself a "thumbs-up" sign (I often use this). Whenever you do it, that is the signal for you to flash your attention to a quiet, serene place where you feel secure and surrounded by love. Notice how your body responds. Once you establish the habit of automatically putting yourself into relaxation mode with your sign, you will have developed a powerful self-help technique. Give this a try as soon as possible to establish the release you can use in many situations and the realization that there is something you can do to manage stress.

9. Consciously Strive to Increase Your Ability to Love

Everyone wants love and approval. Everyone! The vast majority of people I have counseled when grieving were dealing with one basic issue—love. "Am I still loved?" "Am I loveable?" "Will I be loved?" "Who could love me?" "Am I loved from the other side?" They are reluctant to ask these questions outright, but the presentation of their issues points to the perceived lack of this most basic human need.

There is no greater healing energy; your genuine love for others invariably brings love clearly back into the center of your life. Reciprocal love, the common thread in humanity, is the essential factor in meaningful relationships; it is protective and the source of numerous problem-solving insights. You will regain your sense of importance, feel better, and grow through your great loss. It is through that growth that wisdom emerges, adding immeasurably to the quality of your life.

Secrets for Inner Peace

I am convinced that the most effective coping response is increasing your ability to love in whatever you think, say, and do. It is a truism from Virgil that "love conquers all," particularly the pain associated with the death of a loved one and the inner changes it demands in your life. I once heard a famous surgeon say that love was the most powerful immune stimulant known to medicine.

Many counselors and healers appear to have a love for their clients, which seems to speed the healing process. If you choose to love in all instances—and this takes disciplined work—I guarantee it will lead to inner peace.

Nothing will give you more energy or more useful insight into a stress-filled world. The more you live your love, and choose not to let anger dominate, the more you will receive and be able to give away. I have seen it happen again and again.

And yes, putting someone else before yourself is a coping choice you can make even when in pain. It can be the one reliable sanctuary for dealing with all the twists and turns to be faced. As the late psychiatrist Karl A. Menninger of the famous Menninger Clinic said, "Love cures people—both the ones who give it and the ones who receive it." And further, "One does not fall into love; one grows into love, and love grows in him."

As you deal with painful moments, go inside and feel the love you have and have been given. Pause for a moment and consider what experiences of love you have already been given in your dark night. Meditate on those who have loved you through the years and in your present dilemma.

Although you are mourning and feeling sad, here is the key question to address each day and beyond your intense mourning period: how can I put love into *action*? Gentle love speaks in many ways and will increase love for yourself. Here are some beginning approaches other mourners would offer to enable you to build faith in the new world you are facing.

- Tell those who are close to you that you love them, even if you have not verbalized it before.
- Think of ways you can show loving acts of kindness to those who are grieving with you. Decide to become a wounded healer. Be there for others, even though you are actively mourning. Your generosity will lift your energy level and draw a new prosperity into your life.

Be assured, love will keep you afloat whenever the storm within or without seems to be too much to handle; it is *the* life preserver of all life preservers. You only need to sincerely reach for it. That takes commitment. See the world, as well as your nurturing community, as friendly, as people who will be there for you. Spread love as you grieve, and you will draw the comfort you need along the way.

As you work to become more loving, increase efforts to hang out with like-minded people. This will greatly assist in reaching your goal; they will lift your spirits and be examples to follow. When you feel loved, you can get through anything. It has often been said that "Our human choice is not between pain and no pain, but between the pain of loving and the pain of not loving." Healing in life emanates from love and gratitude.

You and you alone can restore joy to your life. No one else can, because you have the power. Let your love be known. As the Spanish mystic Teresa of Avila wrote, "The important thing is not to think much but to love much; and so do that which best stirs you to love."

Widen Your Concept of Love

Love is a decision to relate to all. Love is an active word, a verb that says, "Do what is good." There is nothing I have seen, in all of my years in helping the bereaved, that changes the quality of one's coping ability more than *increasing the ability to love.* Love has an intense, somewhat mysterious self-healing power and guarantees success and adaptation to the new challenges of your life.

Opening your heart wider to all of the people you relate to creates a frame of reference which inspires and at the same time comforts; it is so much more than the romantic version of love that fills the airwaves. You suddenly discover you are not alone in coping with the death of your loved one. Love always goes on. In the arms of love you will find unexpected strength and stamina, a tempering of sadness, and a little less loneliness. You can begin right now by giving it *your highest priority, making it your most important coping response.* Simply be open to it and love will find you.

The blood relatives of genuine love are kindness, empathy, generosity, and especially gratitude. The more you can become a living expression of loving kindness, even as you grieve, the more your grief work will be dominated by thoughts that balance ever-present sorrow; this needed balance cannot be overemphasized. But you have to be specific about the feelings and behaviors that bring that welcomed balance. Affirm all that you have and that you can still do. You will be drawing on your spiritual power and helping yourself through this major transition.

You may be skeptical of this coping method at first, but give it time. Perhaps the least used, yet most powerful action you can take to cope with your loss is to focus on being kind. Even though you are in pain, try to give love. Why? *Because there is no more successful therapy.* If you love, you heal and find your way out of the web of inner turmoil.

YOU ONLY OWE LOVE

It begins with loving yourself; this is an integral part of loving everything. You are intrinsically good. Say it and mean it. You can't really heal without it. Nor can you love others without first loving yourself. Self-love is reflected in treating yourself well every day, specifically your physical, spiritual, mental, and emotional needs. No self put-downs. No berating yourself! This is no small thing.

How can you love yourself?

- Use your strengths. Do what you know you do well.
- Be compassionate toward yourself. That is, be kind to, pamper, and care for yourself, especially when you make a mistake.
- Consider what your loved one loved about you. Can you develop and refine that trait?
- Give yourself credit when you have a good day. And don't wait until the day is perfect; partial successes are extremely important and worthy of credit.
- Make decisions, and celebrate even partial success. These boosts make you feel important and lovable.

> ▸ Volunteer—you will feel better. Give what you need and you will find it. Practice being complementary in the process of interacting with others.
>
> ▸ Think about what you have already accomplished. List accomplishments and review them regularly.
>
> Initially, self-love more than anything else is a choice. Say it: "I love myself. I am a good person." Find a community of love and it will make all of the above much easier to accomplish.

10. Ask for Help after the Funeral or Memorial Service

The first few days of grief are busy and filled with much to do and obligations to fulfill. However, the real work of grieving begins after the funeral, when all the early helpers have retreated into the background and relatives have gone back to their homes. There are not only emotional issues that have to be dealt with but many practical ones as well. Here is where you have to politely be assertive and specific in the kind of assistance you need and when you need it.

Don't Fear the Need to Temporarily Rely on Others

Leaning on others and looking for assistance is something many of us are not familiar with, and it throws many roadblocks in front of our way of life. Even though we are taught to assume responsibility for our behavior and the demands of our roles, grief is one time when we have every right to seek assistance with tasks that normally are exclusively ours. Plus—and this is a big plus—you will give others an opportunity to feel needed in the process.

Consider additional support with new roles and responsibilities, specific information for dealing with finances, or a physical evaluation. You may need help with household chores, taking care of your automobile, or fixing a leaky toilet. If you are a male, you may have to get some shopping tips as well as a few cooking lessons. You may seek help with your children, making travel arrangements, paying bills, getting the estate in order, obtaining food, moving, or any number of tasks. It is okay to be gentle with yourself. Although some work can be useful for your inner life, don't push too hard.

Match your needs to the person best suited to provide the assistance. Sometimes you may have to pay for the expertise of someone who is not a close friend. Ask for recommendations in this regard. It will ease your burden and give peace of mind. By all means don't try to go it alone by holding true to an old belief that was drummed into your head about being totally self-reliant. There are parish nurses, social workers, and hospice volunteers who will provide help with many ongoing responsibilities until you can take complete charge once again. And in the process, there is nothing like learning that others loved your loved one and appreciated his or her contributions.

See Your Doctor

There is nothing wrong with thinking about a trip to the doctor for a check-up. If you consistently feel under the weather with no good days in between, that's a sign. If you have overidentified with your loved one and his or her illness, which is quite normal, and have similar symptoms, that's another sign. You may already feel you are ready for a visit. Perhaps you are having some old injuries flare up due to the strain you are under. Certain illnesses, like colds, influenza, and stomach problems, are associated with bereavement. Is a blood test or other diagnostic test needed? Should an antidepressant be considered? Whatever you determine is necessary, and in conjunction with your physician, then go for it, and set as a priority the direction to better health.

Seeking assistance when you feel overwhelmed is a smart move. We are vulnerable when grieving. Most of us need the insight and inspiration we can receive from those who have the knowledge and experience in dealing with change. Take advantage of their wisdom and the mistakes they learned from to save you time and additional stress.

11. Remember that "Bad Days" Are Normal

Don't be alarmed if you have a difficult day with extreme sadness after you have experienced many good ones. Grief is a roller-coaster. "Bad days" are a normal part of grief work. You are not failing to make headway, so don't start second-guessing yourself.

Make contact with your support system. Tell them what happened. We all need *safe places and safe people*, especially during these times when dark despair starts to creep in and you want to run away from life. You have not failed; it is an opportunity to learn and widen perspective. You are learning about the normalcy of grief. Pick up and begin again, and look at what happened as a result of the normal process of grieving. Know that a "bad day" is only temporary.

Once again, look for someone who tries to understand you and your struggle. The key word here is "tries." Really, can anyone fully understand? I cannot overemphasize that when you feel there is a limited to moderate amount of understanding from a listener, you will have found one of the most powerful forces to spur you on to deal with your loss.

Your loss is extremely significant, and you need to search for those who recognize that fact. To feel understood sets off an inner transformation of immense proportions. You are free to see a different future where you can make a difference. You will continue on the road to healing. Stay away from anyone who trivializes your grief. Such a person knows little about the process, especially the needs of mourners.

12. Place Major Decisions on Hold

This may seem to be a no-brainer. However, many mourners are prone to making decisions about moving, expensive traveling, selling stock, or accepting questionable sales pitches early in their grief. Less-than-sound thinking is another constant companion of the grief process for most. We don't think as clearly as we are capable of when highly stressed.

Emotion and reason often do battle when you are grieving, and regrettably, emotion often ends the winner. In addition, indecision, or making rapid decisions on weighty matters, takes a mighty toll on the healing process. Therefore, take advantage of the experiences of thousands of others who have decided to put major decisions on the shelf in order to give themselves time to strengthen their inner resources and do their grief work. See their wisdom as your wisdom. Take more time, if you are thinking about something such as selling your home and moving right away.

If you are considering going back to work or taking another job, buying a new car, or making any big decision, give yourself time and seek expert input. Ask friends and relatives as well as professionals for their opinion. And remember it's only their opinion. Consider it in the process of decision-making, and then *you* make the decision. Things can look quite different four or five months down the road. At the same time, make decisions based on *your needs*, not on what you feel your loved one would have wanted.

13. Refuse to See Yourself as a Victim

Whenever you talk to yourself or others as though you are a victim, you automatically reduce your ability to cope with your loss. Victims are immobilized and do little to adapt to the conditions imposed by loss. Charles Swindoll says it best: "Cuddle and nurse [self-pity]…and you'll have on your hands in a brief period of time a beast, a monster, a raging, coarse brute that will spread the poison of bitterness and paranoia through your system." This occurs because you have given away your power. It is not unusual to play the victim role when we choose to feel powerless and think we have been wronged.

Connections Are the Greatest Defense

Never surrender to self-pity or despair. Yes, we can feel sorry for ourselves for a few moments but the danger mounts if we linger there. Victims are devoid of the survivor attitude: "I will meet and conquer this great change in my life." Survivors keep on keeping on. They expect to succeed. They search for and make the most of chance opportunities to establish new connections to people, organizations, institutions, clubs, family, their higher power, and friends. In times of adversity your connections, new and old, are most valuable in limiting self-pity.

Why?

Because connectedness heals; it is the pillar of survival, and science has long proved it. We are all one with each other and a higher power. You and I, every person, lives and thrives on the warmth of connections. Keep reinforcing the belief that every living thing is connected. Meditate on it and its implications. You are a part of continual change. Keep telling yourself, "I am working to reduce and eliminate my self-pity." Try the two-minute drill: give yourself two minutes of self-pity, not one second longer, and then take action to change your internal focus.

The collective belief system is fine-tuned to include the belief that there is a greater plan, that we can recognize disempowering roles, and that anyone can turn their great loss into an outcome they can live with—not forget. Maintain and build on your connections, and the transformation you face will be fueled with the inspiration needed to succeed. You will be growing through your loss.

The mourning process will help you, as it has so many, to change self-limiting beliefs. How? By going back and determining how these beliefs were originally formed (when you were young and impressionable) and changing them. Also, by eliminating the sources of negativity that lead to the "I can't do this" automatic thought response. This means to stop focusing on past experiences, meditate each day on the positive things you can do, and stop reading, listening to, or watching anything on television that feeds negative thinking.

Visualize How You Will Cope

Imagine successful coping. Use your imaginal power to discover the web of possibilities that exist, to experience beforehand the various directions you may turn toward in order to face any fear or problem. Then visualize negotiating the difficulties and emotions you face and connecting with the people you know who will inspire your efforts. Every day visualize exactly what you want.

Remember also, comparing your loss to someone else's loss is an exercise in futility. The same is true for comparing one person's grief to another. Don't bother to go there; it only adds to feelings of victimization. Comparisons are a complete waste of time and precious energy. They do nothing but bring unneeded conflict and negativity into your life at a time when your search for meaning demands a positive focus.

You may hear someone say that the loss of a child is the greatest loss, or another say the loss of his/her spouse was so much more difficult because of the nature of the relationship at the time of death. The unvarnished truth is this: each loss is the worst loss for each mourner. There are too many variables involved to think otherwise.

14. Establish a Spiritual Anchor Each Day

Most people do not realize how our mind-set influences our physical health. Use your spiritual resources, which are a huge untapped reservoir of strength. Develop them.

Find a way to start your day on a spiritual note; it will be a motivating boost since spiritual energy is healing. The more you can trade it for the energy drains of anxiety and continuous negative thinking that sap your attempt to get through the day, the more you will gain confidence in your ability to manage grief and, eventually, transform it. Depression, guilt, and anger, though useful, are immense energy sinkholes to deal with as well, and they need to be addressed, sometimes with professional help.

Develop and Honor Your Spiritual Self

Consider beginning the day by acknowledging your higher power with a morning devotion and asking for the strength and wisdom to get through this particular day. Or start the morning by focusing on all that you were able to accomplish up to this point in your grief work. Yes, you have had some successes, if you look carefully.

Perhaps you can refresh your mind by looking at the most important priorities in your life and what you will do on this particular day to honor them. Don't let a day go by without seeking the support of your spiritual reality, as many before you have learned. Your spiritual energy can be renewed each day by learning more about the vast variety of spiritual practices that can be tailored to your values and belief system. Begin the search by talking with those in your circle of friends you feel are spiritually aware.

15. Silence Your Rude and Frightening Inner Voice

Our true inner voice is filled with wisdom and is part of our intuitive self; it is our best adviser. But there is a counter voice, your inner critic, which says things like, "Why did this happen to me? What did I do to deserve this? I can't face all of these changes. I have no future." These lie in your unconscious and come streaming forth from early life experiences. Negative judgments assail you. You dig the hole deeper by letting pessimistic thought-patterns get stronger through repetition, not being fully aware of how they are affecting you. These thoughts reinforce the idea that you can't cope well and accept the reality of your loss. But not this time. Stop beating yourself up. Here's how:

- Decisively take action to change the pattern of thinking and eliminate the specific thought coming from the critic. Immediately say out loud or to yourself: "Stop!" (I often blurt out the word "no," and some use the word "cancel.") As you use the word, envision a big X popping up and cover the thought. Or put a rubber band on your wrist and snap it as you say "Stop!" This is smart self-talk. Do not allow your inner critic to dominate and manipulate. You can choose to transform the thought that has you frozen in fear; it was learned and you can dispatch it. Repeat the word of your choice, again and again, when you become aware of the mental chatter that sends you into a downward spiral.

- Talk back to negative thoughts; do not allow them to control you. Refuse to sit there and take it. Challenge and reject the unwanted thought and make it clear in your mind that you can and will deal with the massive change you face. Think out loud when no one is around, so that you verbalize your positive response to your demons. Make a case for how you have positively dealt with other life difficulties. Don't let self-limiting negativity outtalk you.
- Start doing a chore. Find something that combines your verbal challenge with physical movement. Just do it.
- Use the "act as if" technique discussed in chapter 1 and do something to show that you are in charge. Perhaps you could say an affirmation that condemns the negative and lifts up one of your strengths. Remember, if you are not in charge, your unconscious childhood program is taking over.

Keep your mind set on beating the negative, knowing it will reduce pain and increase your self-confidence as you succeed.

16. Start Loving in Separation

If you want to radically alter the landscape of your life, then embrace the fact that although our loved ones die, love never dies. We are eternally connected through love. The love between you and the person you lost is not frozen in time. You are still loved from the other side and can keep the spirit of your loved one alive in your heart and actions. You do not have to say goodbye. You can actually learn to say "hello" and celebrate the life that has been lived as you continue to move forward in life. Learning to love in separation means many actions on your part. Finding a way to keep your loved one's memory alive forever is a starter.

One of the tasks of grieving is to discover ways to express that eternal connection.

FIND HEALTHY WAYS TO REMEMBER YOUR LOVED ONE

You can strengthen the bonds of love simply by expressing your love in your own creative way. Do something daily, weekly, monthly, or at all special holidays or anniversaries, whatever you prefer. Here is a short list of things other mourners have done to show their love.

- Plant a memorial garden in the spring or tulip bulbs in November in honor of your loved one.
- At home, periodically collect items (canned goods, clothing, etc.) to give to a charity in his/her name. You receive when you give with sincerity.
- Nurture happy life memories for inspiration and to say thanks. Remember that it isn't too late to create new meaningful memories. For example, you could start a new tradition that honors your loved one on a birthday or other significant day.

- Write a history of your relationship with the deceased to be given to your children. Frequently use the qualities and talents the deceased admired in you or brought out in you. Some have also loved well by continuing to work toward reaching certain goals, knowing that the deceased would be so proud when they were attained.

- Share the things received from your association with your loved one. This can be anything from material objects purchased on vacations or special holidays to lessons learned from the way he/she dealt with tasks or problems. Stories about your loved one that illustrate significant character traits are particularly important. These build on the legacy left for others and allow you the needed opportunity to mention his/her name out loud.

- Have an annual church, synagogue, or mosque service in her memory.

- Ask yourself what you have discovered about yourself since the death of your loved one and what action it suggests you take. Are you more compassionate? Do you feel more empathy toward others? Have you learned about your inner strength or personal resources?

- Fund a gift or scholarship given in his/her memory.

- Light a candle in your home on special days as a visible inclusion of the loved one in the day. When alone, focus on the light emanating from the candle and meditate on the symbolic unity meaning it has for your higher power, you, and your loved one. It has often been said, and many believe, that no one ever dies alone or grieves alone.

▸ Perform a dance or sing a song, as many artists do to honor the deceased.

▸ Create a memory box with items belonging to you and your loved one. Tie reminder notes on some of the items to jog your memory.

17. Give and Ask for a Hug

The power of human touch, especially when dealing with loss and change, is not fully recognized in our culture. It is crucial for our well-being; we thrive on it. Of course, there are some people who do not want or like to be hugged. Nonetheless, there is considerable evidence to show that human touch has a positive effect on increasing hemoglobin levels in the blood. Hemoglobin carries vital supplies of oxygen to all of the tissues of the body. Increased hemoglobin means greater oxygenation of vital organs, which can go a long way in maintaining health when under great stress.

The neuropeptide oxytocin is also released through human touch and decreases the level of stress hormones in the body. This is a big reason why cultivating warm, loving relationships is so important throughout life. The health benefits of oxytocin release are far-reaching and include the heart and circulatory system as well as the reduction of inflammation.

Regular hugging, every day if possible, has been shown to affect recovery from reactive depression, help in disease prevention, and add to the great sense of caring that we all need. "Hug therapy" is a big deal. Family therapist Virginia Satir said, "We need four hugs a day for survival. We need eight hugs a day for maintenance. We need twelve hugs a day for growth." Others believe there is a transfer of energy when hugging.

There is nothing untoward about saying, "I could use a hug." It is an apt response if someone asks, "What can I do for you?" or "Is there something I can get you?" If you don't wish to be touched, for whatever reason (you feel vulnerable or embarrassed, have a bad cold, or had a previous bad experience), let it be known at the appropriate time.

These same recommendations apply not only to mourners, but to those who are supporting mourners as well. Sincerely given, a hug can add to developing a positive emotional state as well as an increased sense of security, not to mention a boost in self-esteem. As many have said, a hug is a smile from the heart. You can help others as well as yourself by giving a hug.

And what if you are not the hugging kind, for whatever reason? Then shake hands, or hold hands, give a pat on the shoulder or arm, or kiss as appropriate. Even petting your dog can be beneficial. Nurturing and intimacy are natural ways to cope with loss and change. Human touch is good medicine.

18. Consider Learning EFT

One of the most popular therapeutic methods in energy psychology is called the emotional freedom techniques (EFT), a procedure akin to acupuncture without the needles. Although its origins go back thousands of years, it was developed in its present form by Gary Craig, Stanford engineer and master neuro-linguistic programming (NLP) practitioner. You do not have to believe in the process for it to provide great dividends. In short, you simply tap with your fingertips on various parts of the body to clear blockages in the energy system, what Chinese medicine calls the meridians.

We all have electrical and energy fields, and you already know how your energy is affected by negative emotions and whatever you put into or do with your body. For example, water is a primary conductor of electricity in your electrical system. Little water means reduced energy. I teach the EFT procedure to all of my grief support groups when we discuss the topic of stress management in one of our sessions; I also use it myself in a variety of potentially overwhelming situations. It can be used for physical or emotional pain, including when you are feeling angry, guilty, or depressed. Craig puts it very clearly: "Try it on everything."

At first, the process looks, as one mourner put it, "weird." However, it is an excellent way for anyone to lower the intensity of unnecessary emotional and physical pain, interrupt and clear negative thinking, as well as induce relaxation and reinforce positive behaviors. Yes, all of that and more. I will give you a shortened version here. But you can obtain the entire procedure and start receiving a newsletter by going to http.EFTUniverse.com and a free download of a "how to" manual. This is a self-help tool that will never quit on you.

Energy Points

Here are the energy points to tap on: karate chop point (located in the center of the edge of your hand, where you would make contact if you delivered a karate chop); top of the head (in the center of the head); inner edge of the eye brow (near the bridge of the nose); side of the eye (just past the edge of the eye, toward the temple); under the eye (on the suborbital bone); under the nose (between the nose and upper lip); chin (between the lower lip and bottom of your chin); beginning of the collarbone (where it connects to the breastbone); under the arm (about four inches below the armpit); and the inside of the wrist. Don't be alarmed; after a few practice runs this top-down sequence will become automatic.

The Order for Using EFT/Meridian Tapping

- Try the procedure by first assessing the issue you want to address on a scale from zero to ten, with ten indicating you are feeling the most pain.
- Then use what is called the setup affirmation: "Even though I (insert the problem to tap on), I deeply and completely accept myself." For example, "Even though I feel so angry at

what I didn't do, I still deeply and completely accept myself." Repeat this setup phrase three times and at the same time tap on the karate chop point. Tap with the finger tip of the first or second finger, or both if it feels more comfortable. You can also make up your own setup phrases like "Even though I have this _____, I'm okay with myself" or "I love and accept myself even though I _____."

- Next, go to the top of the head, where you begin to tap on that point seven or eight times. Repeat the same number of taps on each of the succeeding points as described in the paragraph above. Once you memorize the setup affirmation and go through the other eight energy points, you will be on your way to learning this shortened version. And later, you will be able to learn other setup phrases to enhance your ability to benefit from the many uses of EFT.

- The final piece to add is what are called reminder phrases. Using the anger issue again as an example, each time you tap on a point you add a phrase like "feeling so angry" or "angry at myself." It is not essential to use the same reminder on every point.

- Do a minimum of four to five rounds and then assess your intensity level on the zero to ten scale again and compare it to when you started. Repeat as needed.

To summarize, the main parts of this shortened EFT procedure are: (1) Assess the intensity of your problem on a scale from zero to ten. (2) Say the setup phrase three times as you tap the karate chop point. (3) Tap seven or eight times on each of the energy points starting with the top of the head and ending under the arm. (4) Use a reminder phrase as you move from point to point. (5) Assess the level of your pain after doing four to five rounds. Repeat as necessary.

By using EFT, you will develop an invaluable energy-based tool for healing, finding core issues of distress, and limiting beliefs. Its many applications are sure to help you.

19. Be of Service to Others

Whoa, you say. I'm grieving and you want me to be of service to others? Exactly! You are still needed and valuable. Someone needs your eyes to see, your ears to hear, and your arms to be helped. You can change someone's life for the better and in the process find great meaning in your life as you cope with loss.

A universal truth: service to others is the oldest, most effective, and most recommended coping strategy for mourners on the planet. Why? Because the personal power-releasing factor it gives you is hope. Equally important, acts of kindness will keep you socially engaged at a time when you need it most. Sharing has always been an anxiety reducer.

From Me to We

Make every effort to avoid living too long in a self-centered world, because it will add to your inability to create the inner life most conducive to relieving suffering. *Focus on people*. Believe, as many before you have experienced, that if you give to the world, the world gives back to you tenfold. Practice hospitality in the lives of others in the best way possible: giving them hope by your presence and commitment. Come to know the joy of committed service. Everyone wants to be acknowledged, valued, and celebrated.

Share Time, Talent, and Treasure

Never underestimate the power of your actions. One small gesture of giving can change a life. If you want to heal and feel good about yourself and at the same time see yourself as a contribution to the world, follow this ancient but most productive advice: Give more than expected; you can't go wrong. Once you commit yourself fully to making a positive influence in the lives of others, it is easy to continue to use your talents and find relief from pain. Focus on selfless action rather than unhealthy obsession that prolongs suffering. Here is a short list to get you started:

- Give some items of clothing to Goodwill or the Salvation Army.
- Find someone who is without transportation and needs a ride to town and back.
- Volunteer to visit someone at your local nursing home.
- Feed the birds.
- Send thank-you notes to the friends who have helped you thus far.
- Go to the grocery store for someone who has difficulty shopping.
- Send a sympathy card or recommend a book to read to someone you know who is a newly bereaved person.

- Be the first to say hello and give a smile to the people you meet. Acknowledging others gives them a boost.
- Offer to let someone go ahead of you when waiting in line.
- Help out a bit more at home with chores, more than is normally expected.
- Teach something you do well to someone else. You are a major contribution. And don't forget to teach others, in due time, what you have learned about grief and grief work.
- Give your full attention when speaking to family, friends, or strangers; in reality, you will be showing love for them.

You can think of many more. Make a long list to keep as a reminder when you are struggling to come up with selfless acts to perform. Earn and be a focus of the gratitude of others. Make it a priority every day to be an influence in the lives of others by focusing on how you will make them feel good, and you will find another opportunity to reinvest in life. Ralph Waldo Emerson said, "It is one of the beautiful compensations of this life that no one can sincerely try to help another without helping himself."

Give someone the gift of your knowledge, a sincere compliment, or a sense of importance by your attention. Or offer caring encouragement. The rewards never fail to surface. The less you think about yourself, the more great things you can do.

After performing good deeds, people are happier and feel their life has more purpose. Give yourself a gift through giving. Spreading your light will lift the dark veil.

20. Find Release and Comfort in Writing

Over two decades ago, a young woman wrote me the following: "I think it is of ultimate importance to always have someone to listen to you when you are depressed about anything. I have what I call my Nothing Book and it is a book full of blank pages. When I am upset and have no one to talk to, I write everything I am feeling in the book. Sometimes I write it in the form of a letter to the person I am upset with, and it makes me feel like I got it off my chest."

How you wear your grief on a daily basis has an awful lot to do with your awareness of the need to find ways to naturally let it keep flowing. The mounting evidence that the act of writing is a major therapeutic release is impressive. Putting your thoughts and feelings on paper is a catharsis recommended by psychologists and psychiatrists worldwide for a variety of emotional ills and to better understand your inner world.

The consistent use of writing is one of the most effective and least used ways to manage the pain of grief. It will help you physiologically, especially in your immune system, as well as emotionally, according to Dr. James Pennebaker of the University of Texas at Austin. Allowing feelings created by your thoughts to flow from your head, down through your hand, and on to paper is a releasing process in itself. You may want to keep a journal that you write in at a particular time each evening or whenever you feel overwhelmed by feelings that need to be expressed. It helps to put on some comforting music or write near a picture of the person you are mourning.

Here is where you tell it like it really is, with all honesty, not the way you think a friend would be able to take it. Forget about correct spelling or exact punctuation. Just make sure your text is readable because you will benefit immensely by coming back later to read what you boldly penned. Weeks or months down the road you will see where you were, how far you have come, and who you are now becoming. You will gain perspective and an understanding of life that you did not possess previously. As another grieving mother put it, "Time doesn't heal all wounds, but it gives us the opportunity to gain perspective about our loved one, and ourselves, and that is what heals us." This is a wise observation.

Use the journal to write your specific daily goals, either the night before or the first thing in the morning. The key word here is "specific." Identify exactly what you want to get through and how you will do it as the day unfolds. Start small. Believe you will achieve your goals. Or make a task list. In the evening, check to see what you did in comparison to what you wanted to do on that particular day. Decide where you need to change behavior or try something different.

If your self-image (the way you think about yourself) has plummeted due to your loss—not an unusual occurrence—write about the little successes you have had during the day, and at the close, slip in a positive affirmation that hits home. How you see yourself has a major impact each day on how you adapt to loss, whether you are on the way out of pain or driving yourself deeper into turmoil. Bottom line: with consistent work, you can change your self-image and in the process affect the course of your grief work through your pen.

Some mourners find it helpful to write at the time when they have a sudden upsurge of grief (a grief attack) or whenever another loss triggers memories of a previous loss. Say what is natural for you at the time of your writing. Express the unthinkable. Confess your faults. It may also be helpful for falling asleep to jot down what you are feeling each evening before you retire. Talk about feeling loved or unloved. Or write poems or eulogies. If you climb in bed and start thinking of something else, get up and write it down so you can quiet your mind and get to sleep.

This mode of self-expression is not merely an excellent way to process and release conscious feelings. Some thoughts and feelings are in the unconscious and you may not be fully aware of them or their effects. Yet writing often stimulates unconscious thought processes, and these hidden thoughts and feelings will surface to be aired and better understood. Here is an example from Anne, who said, "I am not a writer, but this came flying out of my fingers."

> *It seems to me that all of our problems, tragedies,*
> *   difficulties, and*
> *crises are the opportunity to be sprinkled or doused*
> *   with spiritual*
> *fertilizer. Thus our roots multiply and go deeper into*
> *   the living water.*
> *Our branches expand upward to God and sideways*
> *   to others and some*
> *criss-cross toward the center and have to be pain-*
> *   fully but necessarily pruned*

> *to redirect them outward. Our leaves take on a*
> *healthy glow for all to see.*

All of the above lay hidden in the vast resource of her unconscious mind, which records all past thoughts and experiences. How long it was within, and what triggered it to come out in the form in which it was expressed, no one knows.

Last, if it seems right for you, consider taking the journal with you if you visit the cemetery or wherever the remains of your loved one have been placed. Once there, write what you feel.

21. Don't Allow Excessive Attention to Prolong Mourning

Sometimes, depending on the nature of the loss, an amazing outpouring of sympathy and assistance overpowers the bereaved. The continuous attention given by friends and family often aids and abets the self-pity already generated by the mourner. The person believes that his or her loss is the worst there can be (as most of us do) and nothing can be done to assuage the grief. The first may well be true. The second—never. Loss becomes the central focus of life as the mourner constantly relives the terrible scene of the loss and expects ongoing, never-ending assistance. If you feel you are getting too much attention, make it clear that you need time alone, whether during the day or in the evening. How? In a sincere and appreciative way, tell your support persons you are so thankful for their presence and help. Tell them you love them and will always need their friendship. Follow your heartfelt thanks with the request that you begin to deal with some of your new routines by yourself at certain times.

If you refuse to let go of a portion of your sadness—another choice—you are sealing yourself into a self-made prison for the rest of your life. It is in the here and now, right now, that you will make progress, by yourself as well as with others. This does not mean you are supposed to forget your loved one or move at the pace of your support persons. Not at all. What it implies is that you must establish a new loving relationship with the deceased based on memory and tradition as you rebuild your life. We all tell our stories through memory.

All of this takes courage. The good news is you can turn to your best friend, clergy, higher power, counselor, therapist, or social worker for help to act, to speak, to heal. You possess the power to begin a different course. Carlos Castaneda reminds us that "Any path is only a path, and there is no affront to oneself or to others, in dropping it if that is what your heart tells you."

Do not allow death to be a source of self-pity, what counselors call a big part of secondary gain. When a mourner self-pities, they often receive comforting responses or attention from others. As a result, some people would rather stay in a perpetual grief state than face the challenges of life without the loved one. You can escape that trap, which narrows your life and feeds the need for external validation, by taking small painful steps to enter your new world.

22. Finish Unfinished Business

It is not unusual to have unfinished business with the loved one who died, especially if the death was unexpected. Ambivalent feelings are a part of most relationships. It may be something that was left unsaid or something that you did or did not do and now feel angry or guilty about. Or there was an event precipitated by the loved one that could have been resolved, and you are angry about it. But it is never too late to complete the task of making amends.

Initially, it is necessary to find someone you trust to talk about whatever is bothering you. Don't keep it a secret. Friends are emotional outlets. Ask for an opinion. Then decide what you need to do to attain inner peace and forgive or seek forgiveness. Never hold anyone hostage to the past, for in reality you are only holding yourself in prison.

Many resolve unfinished business by doing the following:

- Find a quiet place where you can speak out loud to the deceased. This could be the cemetery, the lake, any place.
- Be specific about what is causing your inner turmoil and speak about it to the deceased. Then put yourself in the other person's place. Imagine your loved one hearing your words. Imagine what he or she would say back to you.
- After you speak, pause and remain quiet. Examine the thoughts that pop into your mind. If you feel you have been a victim, say so. Say what you need to say to ease your burden and reduce emotional baggage.

- Believe you have been heard. Look for signs within and without.
- You may also want to try doing any of the above with someone you trust, to be there to listen, to witness.

It can also be useful for you to create a ritual of forgiveness. Follow any of these approaches by going for a brisk walk, which will further reduce the physical effects of dealing with your anxiety. What *you* do, no one else, to change the way you relate to unfinished business with your loved one is the key to resolution.

23. Use Rituals to Cope with Your Transition

Formal and informal ritual promotes connection to the deceased and helps survivors by giving support, facilitating transition, and providing comfort. Ritual connections help establish an important pathway to accepting loss, establishing a new relationship with the deceased. Small ritual moments can bring large inner blessings. I know one woman who began an informal ritual of saying good morning to her deceased husband as she passed by his photograph upon rising. She then went on about her day, content that she had acknowledged him, and she realized in her heart that love still connected them.

Rituals can be something you do every day, week, month, or year with the intent of honoring the loved one and knowing he or she will never be forgotten. You decide the extent and frequency.

Words need not be expressed out loud in whatever ritual you begin, nor do they necessarily have to be spoken within. An action alone, touching a flower or other object, walking through a particular room or outside area, may be just as meaningful for you. It is the intent and the symbolic meaning that count and that can help you move through another day and regain your strength.

Formal rituals can also prove extremely useful. Funerals and memorial services provide opportunities for all to publicly participate in honoring and celebrating the deceased. The formal ritual on an anniversary, birthday, or other special day provides an opportunity to say thanks, with friends (or alone), for a life lived and to establish the continued importance of the loved one to you. Some plan rituals around weddings and graduations, or when one decides to take a wedding ring off his/her finger. The person will always be a significant part of your life history, and you honor that significance and the love that binds you together with each ritual expression.

CREATE A RITUAL JUST FOR YOURSELF

In thinking about rituals to honor your loved one, don't forget to design one or two to honor yourself. It can be anything you do as part of relieving the daily anxiety you are under. It could be visiting your favorite coffee shop each morning, a sauna in the evening, or reading a chapter from one of your favorite books each day. Make whatever you do a part of the new you reaching out to yourself.

24. Plan Something to Look Forward To

A healthy way to release the constant focus on your great loss is to incorporate a highlight to look forward to into your daily and/or weekly schedule. This should be something that you feel strongly about that brings a measure of joy and satisfaction. It will be one of the high points of your day. Take the time in the evening to go to a quiet place and with paper and pencil jot down three things you will look forward to doing on each of the next three days. On the evening of the third day, write down three more for the next three days. Plan ahead for the month with other events you know are scheduled. Look at your calendar for potential conflicts so that those people you call on are not already committed to another social function or obligation.

These special highlights should not be the usual diversions, like painting or mowing the lawn, to keep busy, but ones that are at the top of your want list. It might be visiting your most trusted friend that you really feel comfortable being around. It could be taking a bubble bath, seeing your grandchildren, using a highly developed skill you possess, or taking a one-day boat trip. Think of the things you want to accomplish that will *lift you up*, that you can think ahead about, and that will give encouragement. Some will appear as you are doing what you had planned the day before, or you may get an idea from watching television. But make it special to give a glimmer of hope for the next day. Remember that the focus of this exercise is on releasing the constant focus on grief and in no way demeans the nature of your grieving.

25. Normalize the Physical Responses of Grief

You don't grieve just in your thoughts. Though often a neglected piece of wisdom, the fact is that the mind—and what we think—rules the body. The universal law is: *what you think and feel creates the intensity and reality in which you grieve.* For every thought and emotion we hold, there is a corresponding physical manifestation of that thought or emotion in *every* cell in the body. In short, thoughts and moods produce stress-related physical symptoms.

Although a degree of distress is not uncommon, sadness and sorrow will be expressed throughout the body in painful ways. Headaches, digestive disturbances, stress-related disorders of sleep and fatigue, and various aches and muscle pains are not uncommon when grieving. The degree of physical discomfort is directly proportional to the constant sad and hopeless thoughts you dwell on without deliberately deciding to take a break. Overeating comfort food or not eating enough are additional factors that may add to physical discomfort. You can break the vicious cycle.

How do you normalize physical responses? First, recognize how your thoughts and actions are contributing to how you feel. Then consciously accept the fact that some of those physical feelings are to be expected given your great loss. Don't discredit yourself for having these unwanted feelings. However, you can divert your attention from them and reduce the intensity of the automatic physical response. Let your awareness of physical pain be the signal to focus attention in another direction by starting a conversation, doing a chore, or engaging in whatever activity that allows you a diversion. Dwell on this key understanding: what you focus on expands. Look for something to renew and refresh your thoughts for a while. As you begin to accept your loss and eat well, your physical pain will lessen.

26. Acknowledge Depression and Give Up the Old for the New

It is common and quite normal to experience reactive depression when you are fearful and to believe that life has no meaning because your loved one has died. Depression is a sign that we are emotionally depleted, with a sense that there is no place to go. The late psychiatrist Scott Peck wrote that depression is our inability to give up the old for the new. And that is exactly what grieving is all about, giving up the way life used to be with our special person and adapting to a different life. No one likes the fact that there is no choice in this regard, except living in the past. We have to transform the old involving our loved one (not forget him or her) and replace it with new behaviors to adapt to the present. It is a change from the old relationship to a new relationship.

There is nothing wrong with being depressed. It signals you to take a time-out and listen carefully to what's happening inside and discuss it. You will learn more about yourself, your needs, and your transition.

So how might you proceed? Acknowledge the fact of depression, instead of resisting. You are not weak, and there is nothing to be ashamed of. Next, don't keep your depression to yourself. You need human contact; depression will deepen without it. Tell someone you trust, who will let you ramble on and just be with you. If you stuff it down, that is, repress your feelings of loss, you increase depression. Talk about them, feel their pain in various forms, and let them go through you.

In a lot of cases, depression is linked to internalizing stressful events, ruminating about the past, and not regularly using common stress-release techniques. This is another reason human contact is so important. The link between depression and stress also implies that you should grab any chance to move: exercise is by far one of the most effective ways to treat reactive depression. Try exercising outside, on a walking or hiking tail; nature is another proven form of relief. Dr. James S. Gordon, MD, a world-renowned expert on depression, has said: "What we're finding in the research on physical exercise is that *exercise is at least as good as antidepressants* for helping people who are depressed."

Another line of management is to find something that will refresh you and help deal with the transition. Constantly keep in mind that you alone control what goes on within, but have little or no control of what happens out there. Regular activities requiring your presence will be a factor in reducing or preventing long bouts of reactive depression. The key word is *regular*. Force yourself to develop outside interests, a project, or a service where you must be around people. And let your depression do what it will.

27. Mourn at Your Own Pace

One of the salient characteristics of grief is that it manifests in a variety of different ways. It has different rhythms and intensities. It can't be directed like a stage play, to pander to the audience. It works at its own pace—your pace, not your neighbor's, or that of any other part of your support system. Refuse to be manipulated. Never grieve according to the agenda of a friend or family member who urges you to do this or that. You alone know the pace, how it feels, what you need, when to shift gears.

This is not easy to accomplish, as you will have to deal with the reactions of others to your decision to grieve as you see fit. This does not mean that you spurn all advice. Listen with respect and decide what is usable for you.

If at some point you are convinced you are stuck in your grief (after several months), see an expert on the grief process. Write up your list of questions before you go. Don't just go to anyone who does counseling. Look for a professional whose primary counseling load is with people who are grieving. They can give invaluable advice that will save you fruitless days and sleepless nights. As one example, consult the Association for Death Education and Counseling (www.adec.org) for grief counselors in your area. They can help you uncover your strengths, myths that are prolonging grief, and remove the obstacles to reducing the intensity of grief. *Always go to professionals who are recognized experts on grief.*

28. Schedule Activities to Get You through Weekends

One of the most common complaints I have heard from those who are mourning is the difficulty of getting through weekends, when they have so much time on their hands. One effective way to deal with this weekly event is to begin scheduling weekend activities outside the home in advance. Do your grocery shopping on Saturday morning. Try the farmer's market in your area. Plan a weekly drive on Sunday to a nearby destination. Visit botanical gardens. Check your local newspaper for events that are scheduled that you might be interested in. Check in with your children.

These, as well as specific entertainments, are all part of your new routines. More important, meaningful and pleasurable activities have been shown to lead to a greater sense of well-being. Start your search right away for things you can do, especially activities you haven't tried before. And don't forget to look for activities that are free or inexpensive.

Make a list of the people who might be available on weekends whom you can befriend. Ask them to go along on a new adventure—the perfect remedy for play deprivation. Sometimes others have similar problems with weekend loneliness and will welcome your inquiry. It's doing something that counts, even if it doesn't work out the way you thought it would. Keep at it and try something new in that time slot next week.

29. Forget Perfect

No one copes with the death of a loved one without feeling some sense of inadequacy. Coping well is not about perfection; it's about love, mistakes, learning, and grudgingly accepting the new. Over time, the new becomes the norm, still different but more livable than we thought it could be. Now, to get to this place takes lots of bumps and bruises. If you happen to be a perfectionist or a control freak, and fail to realize that grieving is not a process of perfect choices and behaviors, your suffering will increase. In fact, there is no such thing as perfect grieving or a perfect life. So dump the word "perfect."

You aren't always going to say the right thing, feel good, or do the right thing. Keep aiming to go forward and make progress. Yes, you will slip back on occasion. Remember those "grief attacks." That's when you gather your courage, get up, and get started again. Take note of what brought you down, and make an effort to avoid what can be avoided. If you are doing something that keeps causing you pain and problems, even if you expect a different outcome, it just won't happen. Try something new immediately, even if it is hard to get started; it will take you out of being in the same place with the same pain.

And don't expect perfection from your support community, your best friend, your spiritual advisor, your counselor, or your spouse or children. Accept the normal mistakes that we humans tend to make in relationships. The only thing the perfect friendship myth will do for you is maximize loneliness.

30. Establish Time for Grief and Worry

Establishing a specific time to do much of your grieving and/or worrying can be one of the most strategic moves you can make when mourning. Why? Because it will cut into the often continuous flow of sadness that intrudes throughout the day. Worrying is the most common way we increase the pain of loss and block clear thinking. Worry all you want—within limits.

Having a set time, when you really allow it all to come out, will give you the option to postpone some nagging heartaches and give you some release from the relentless bombardment of victimizing thoughts. Then you can more fully accept your broken heart.

Once a daily time has been established and you think of a hurtful thought, you can say to yourself or out loud, "I will deal with that at my worry time." You have freed yourself in the present moment to go on with what you were doing, and this is perfectly legitimate. If need be, write it down, and it may be easier for you to let it go temporarily.

When "worry time" comes, deal with it. Find a private place. Surround yourself with objects that remind you of your loved one, cry or express emotions, and talk as you see fit. Here is where you can take inventory of your greatest stressors, fears, and concerns. Think about how you will deal with those that are most demanding. Whom should you contact? Where can you get assistance? Pretest solutions at this time. And if you miss your scheduled worry time, for whatever reason, that's good, since most worries are total exaggerations anyway. Just schedule it for the next day.

Perhaps you may need nothing more than to give yourself permission to fully feel the pain of your great loss at worry time. Or perhaps you really need to think of all the good memories. Anticipate this time each day, so you can get out whatever is in your thoughts. You decide how long you need, though I recommend not going longer than thirty minutes. Talk as you would normally talk. When time is up, stop and have something planned that you will do: some chore inside or outside the home, or a pleasant event to break up the day.

There is nothing wrong with giving yourself this opportunity to put your attention on other needs. Many people have used this approach to get through the day, take care of practical matters, and interact with others.

31. Find Physical Outlets for Emotional Stimuli: Exercise

Yes, I know you've heard this one before. But stay with me. Healthy habits consistently disappear when we are grieving. Whatever you do, don't minimize or reject the major contribution exercise can make to your ability to adapt to the changes imposed by your loss. There's an overwhelming amount of evidence clearly showing that exercise is absolutely essential for optimal emotional and physical health.

First and foremost, you need a physical outlet for all of the tension that has been built up in your body due to the way loss is processed. These feelings are stored in muscle. The evidence is abundantly clear: exercise, particularly brisk walking, will promote sleep, reduce depression (helps prevent it as well), relieve neuromuscular hypertension, and decrease anxiety. It also slashes the incidence of some forms of cancer.

Many psychiatrists say that walking is just as good as Zoloft or other antidepressants. Perhaps most important, exercise can improve your resistance to fight infections by giving your immune system a boost. It also has a positive ripple effect on energy levels, as well as quickly metabolizing the arousal hormones that give you that uptight feeling.

If you are bummed by the thought of starting an exercise program, know that it will *provide relief from emotional pain.* Especially try green exercise—anything you do outside in nature—like gardening, walking, jogging, or biking, where you can take your mind off the feeling of exercise as work and simply enjoy the beauty around you.

Use exercise (if possible, do some running, but hopefully at least a good walking program) to increase the levels of "feel good" endorphins (natural painkillers). Even walking a dog will be helpful. The benefits of consistent exercise are huge in comparison to the time it takes from your day.

If you are completely turned off by exercise, try this: the first day, just do three minutes. You can spare that. The next day, add three more. Stay at six minutes for the next three days. Then, begin to add three more minutes each day, until you are doing thirty minutes a day. Be assured: you will definitely feel better over time. But you must be regular in your workouts and follow a good nutrition program. It will help if you can find someone to exercise with you. The development of strength, endurance, and concentration—mental fitness—will surprise you.

32. Stop Anticipating Old Routines

It's scary to see our old ways going, going, gone, drifting off into the past. However, few things are more self-defeating than anticipating old routines that involved your loved one, when deep inside you know they can't be repeated. When the expected inter-action between the two of you can no longer occur, to focus your attention on what used to be is to invite unnecessary suffering. When you begin to replay that five o'clock drink together, shopping with him on Saturday morning, or that weekend stroll in the park, make a plan to substitute for these routines. Instead, change the timetable you had, at least temporarily, to give yourself time to assimilate the new. Have your drink later in a different location in your home, go shopping on Friday evening, and walk in the park in the morning before work.

Embracing new routines is a giant step forward, as difficult as it may be, because it demands that you step outside of your comfort zone. Know that eventually you can gradually settle into this new way of life. Examine your daily routines that included your loved one, choose the ones that have been most painful, and determine what you can substitute or change, one routine at a time. Starting an entirely new routine is also appropriate and often necessary as you adapt.

33. Learn What Fuels a Toxic Mind-Set

Anything that takes away from your goal of peace of mind and the control of ANTs (automatic negative thoughts) has to be recognized and confronted. For example, are you fully aware of the people in your social circle or family who often say the wrong thing at the wrong time—and cause additional suffering and turmoil? Can you feel their hovering scrutiny and negative energy engulf you? Reduce your exposure to these people as much as possible. The emotional contagion they bring takes away the positive energy you need to deal with each day.

The same is true for toxic places and memories. Become aware of what sets you off. You may not be ready to pass by the location where your loved one died. Later, but not now. It's okay to take a different route and save yourself the additional anxiety and the memories that fuel it. This is not being weak; it's using your mind as a form of preventive care and reducing a toxic mind-set. Make it a spiritual practice. I cannot overemphasize the impact toxic people and places can have on your attitude and how you grieve. You have a duty to yourself to minimize contact with these conflicts as much as possible.

If your loved one died at home, it might be difficult for you to go into that particular room for a while or see a familiar piece of furniture. You can avoid the anxiety it generates by simply not going in there or putting the furniture in a different arrangement. Later, you will find that the pain of going into that room will begin to lessen.

Stressors are always going to be forcing their way unexpectedly into your thought life, even when things seem to be going well. We can't eliminate their sudden appearance, but we sure can smack them down. You can counter the assault by creating a program ahead of time to replace the one you keep replaying and, in the process, elevate a positive mood.

If there are objects that cause you pain to look at, put them away for awhile. Make the deliberate decision to identify what brings negative feelings into your life or increases your sadness. Then decide how to reduce and hopefully eliminate the repetition of these events until you are better prepared to deal with them. Negative feelings are more prevalent and tend to dominate the journey through grief, highly influencing attitude and perceptions. Make the effort to dispatch them by changing the circumstances that promote toxic behavior and directing attention toward life-affirming action.

AN EXERCISE TO PROMOTE INNER PEACE

Use the Lake Placid approach. When you want inner peace, choose a peaceful scene to pour all of your attention into and dispel the toxic mind-set. Picture a mirror-like body of water with a person at the tiller of a small sailboat. Focus first on the smooth surface that glimmers in the sunlight. As the bow of the boat cuts the surface of the water, stay focused on the pointed ripple of the wake. Now see it get smaller and smaller as it spreads out and the boat moves onward. Watch the wake dissolve back into the mirror-like surface. Keep the picture and the calmness of the scene alive and see yourself becoming part of the peaceful-ness returning to the lake. Play the same scene and vary your location by first seeing yourself sitting on a dock, then on a hill by the sea, or on the deck of a cruise ship.

34. Utilize Quotations in Your Healing Process

Quotes are powerful sources of inspiration. Among my favorites that I have often written and spoken of is by Alfred Einstein: "The probability of life originating by accident is comparable to the probability of the unabridged dictionary resulting from an explo-sion in a print shop." This holds great meaning for me, which I will get back to in a moment. What is important to understand here, and what can help you in healing, is that great minds can give you ideas so that you see your loss differently, reframe it, or as the psychotherapists say, "gain perspective on your problem." That is, create a mind-set or attitude change.

The goal is to see your loss in a host of different ways and utilize the wisdom of those who have gone before us. Google the words "grief quotations," for example, and see what you come upon.

These quotes are intended to be practical and useful, not eso-teric. They could well be eye-openers that will help your inner growth in facing the difficult. Here are some examples of what you can find as you step into the shoes of your heroes.

When you are sorrowful look again in your heart, and you shall see that in truth you are weeping for that which has been your delight.

—KAHLIL GIBRAN

Give sorrow words; the grief that does not speak whispers the o'er-fraught heart and bids it break.

—WILLIAM SHAKESPEARE

Even hundredfold grief is divisible by love.

—JAREB TEAGUE

If you're going through hell, keep going.

—WINSTON CHURCHILL

Death is not extinguishing the light; it is putting out the lamp because the dawn has come.

—RABINDRANATH TAGORE

You can clutch the past so tightly to your chest that it leaves your arms too full to embrace the present.

—JAN GLIDEWELL

Every evening I turn my worries over to God. He's going to be up all night anyway.

—MARY C. CROWLEY

Many of these quotes give us resources to meditate on. Read and reread your quotes and mull over them for best results. Back to my interpretation of Einstein's quote. Here's how it speaks to me. Because I feel and believe that there is a supreme being, I can lean on divinity for support and direction. I know I will always be loved and will be given what I need to make it through my terrible times when my loved ones die. I keep asking for assistance and somehow it arrives. Find the right quotes for you. Have them framed or buy them already framed, and place them on your desk, bed stand, or wall as a constant reminder of what to do and how to meet your goals.

35. Accept Cognitive and Mental Distortions

Not infrequently, when you're grieving, you may experience a variety of temporary cognitive and mental changes that add to your already heavy burden of sadness. *Cognitive* refers to the process of knowing—the key word is "process"—while *mental* implies existing in the mind. Among the most frequently reported, is the inability to concentrate on a topic, from reading a book to following the gist of a conversation. One woman said early in her grief, "I couldn't even read the newspaper." This is not an abnormal reaction. Your attention span may be all but nonexistent, and you forget common facts that normally would be easily recalled.

Disordered, even irrational thinking, is not uncommon.

You also may not be able to put together ideas and concepts and quickly come to a conclusion on the next step to take. Mourners sometimes become forgetful and feel they are losing their minds. It is not unusual to be in a state of shock after the death of a loved one and have no recollection of parts of the memorial service, meeting certain friends, or of what you did or did not do the day before. Others forget what they did with their keys or important documents. Once again, for many this is simply due to the shock and numbness of the grief process. Accept it and rely on others for awhile. Most importantly, forgive yourself for not remembering.

Sometimes strong anger or heavy neurotic guilt is behind distorted thinking patterns. And don't be alarmed if you find yourself believing your loved one is temporarily away or that you are looking at your loss through the eyes of a child. Although most of these bothersome events occur early in the grief process, some may carry over for longer periods of time. Be patient with yourself and ask for help in your recall, as difficult as that may be. The greatest majority of bereaved persons do not need professional counseling, and this confusion will eventually lift. If you feel you need help—seek it.

36. Build Your Confidence

Doing what is new won't always feel terribly uncomfortable—if you consistently practice. There are no quick fixes in facing the unfamiliar and adapting to all of the changes involved. But you can get through anything, if you lay out the route you know you have to follow, and practice the steps you will have to take. This is what positive thinking is all about—learned behavior that you continually repeat.

Each time you do the new, you are building a positive thinking style. Repetition is a powerful confidence builder. Here's how to begin the task.

- Create a vision board (a collage of images and affirmations) from pictures clipped from magazines and put them on your bulletin board or a poster board. Use pictures and sayings that represent the way you want to deal with each day or that suggest specific goals you wish to meet.
- Place it in a spot that you will pass by each day as you prepare breakfast.
- See yourself doing the specific behavior and say to yourself or out loud, "I can do it." Tell a best friend your goals and be open to reminders. Type them on your computer screen so you see them every day. Decide to move on this. Don't procrastinate.

Imagined rehearsal will combat toxic worry and give you confidence when the time comes and you have to take action on your goals. Practice in a safe environment and, if applicable, ask friends to assist or give you feedback before you actually try your new response. Feedback from the right people who are knowledgeable will be an important asset and motivator in dealing with changes that have to be made. You can overcome fear with the help of a friend and initiate your new behavior.

37. Search for New Meaning in the Death of Your Loved One

Death is consistently a giver of meaning. It causes us to take a look at what is really important in life and develop and maintain our existing relationships. It always causes us to think about our own death and ask why our loved one had to die. An important question to consider in coping with your great loss is: can I find meaning in the death of my loved one and what other meanings are possible? Death challenges our faith and beliefs and frequently spurs growth in survivors.

Nonetheless, the death of our loved ones may also bring a crisis of meaning, where life seems to lose purpose and direction. Examine where you are in your grief and what you now question about life, death, sorrow, and your belief system. What new perspectives or fears have slipped into your thinking? What personal and/or symbolic meaning has the death had for you? What meanings have changed? Talk about these possibilities with a confidant. Consider if there has been any difference in the way you relate to the death of your loved one. And it is quite possible that you may not be able to find meaning in the death. Instead, there may be a reevaluation of meaning to confront. You may have to go on living knowing that the conflict exists and that at some point in life your search may or may not culminate in meaning-making.

The reconstruction of meaning in life after the death of a loved one always evolves from the connections we have and focusing on what *is*. As meanings change throughout life, we have to discover new meaning. You are still and always will be connected to your deceased loved one. Forever! How can you celebrate that connection? If you have received a sign or message from your loved one, use it as a way to strengthen meaning and belief in your spirituality as you establish your new relationship with him or her. Know that the person you love lives on, knows what you are going through, and that reunion will occur.

Oh, and don't forget, it has long been known that we tend to underestimate the importance of meaning. It dramatically alters physiology and the way we cope with our loss. It highly influences the ability to endure, heal, or create. And it often guarantees safe passage through massive change. Above all, it is *the* pivotal force in all of our relationships. Enough said.

38. Learn Early On What Wastes Energy

Everyone has an energy field. When you are bursting with energy, and you have people with positive energy around you, you know how it feels. You are up and at 'em. You can take a lot and it doesn't break you down as quickly as when your energy level is on low or empty. Often, what doesn't bother you in the morning becomes a problem later in the day, when you're tired. Listen carefully to your body, as suggested earlier. It can give you much input on changing inner thoughts that will positively affect emotions. Working with your emotions—which are incredible powerhouses—will add to or take away from your energy levels.

Most important: physical and emotional pain, and holding emotions in, takes huge amounts of energy.

The Power of Thought

Learn what your energy sinkholes are and what restores these depleted sources. It is all tied to thoughts. You already know that what you allow to stay in your thoughts, as well as the people and the energy you are around, clearly affects the way you feel. I said earlier that toxic people and places are strong energy drainers. Reduce contact with them, and be extremely selective in what you allow to linger in your thoughts. The way you talk to yourself, coupled with anger and fear, is also a big drain if you are critical of yourself.

On the other hand, positive inner dialogue sustains energy, depending on what you do and say. Drop the words "never" and "I must" at this stage of mourning. "Hope," "love," "faith," and "optimism" are all big plus words, and it is wise to say and call on them regularly. Use your spiritual resources to tap into the above and decrease inner conflict. Above all, honor your values if you have a tendency to compromise them. In doing so, you will plug a huge source of lost energy.

There is much that you can do to power up and meet the obligations and new demands of each day to facilitate healing. Frequently close your eyes and relax in a chair as you consider the options, good as well as risky, that are available on a given problem. Examine how your body responds to one choice or another.

Use this relaxing wisdom. Review daily activities and decide what helped your energy level and what depleted it. Start deleting the thoughts and actions that are dragging you down. Keep paying attention to what it feels like inside—a drain or a freeing up, light feeling, or an energy lift. Listen carefully for the subtle cues. This is another great resource to consult in making decisions for peace of mind. And don't forget to increase contact with people who make you feel secure and grounded—all energy conservers.

ESSENTIALS FOR BOOSTING ENERGY

Here are three things to do every day that will raise your energy level as they have mine. In every support group I conduct, I emphasize these as part of self-care. Make the decision to keep self-care a priority and reduce physical pain and discomfort.

Drink Plenty of Water

Although specific water amounts needed differ with individuals, drink a minimum of five eight-ounce glasses of spring water daily, alkalized if possible. This is not a great deal of water. Measure eight ounces and see how small an amount it is. Yet the vast majority of Americans are unknowingly chronically dehydrated. Mourners are even more prone to dehydration as many drink more coffee, soda, or alcohol than usual due to the stress of grieving. Dehydration and water absence heavily contributes to fatigue, headaches, physical pain, and confusion. Most do not realize that water is one of the best pain relievers, energy restorers, and preventive therapies in all of medicine, though hardly publicized.

Therefore, don't miss the body's daily water need; water is the universal lubricant, the basis for all life, and every cell craves it, especially when stressed. Drink water on schedule before you feel thirsty. As unusual as it may sound, make water an integral part of your personal grief therapy. Oh, and don't forget, soda, coffee, and tea do not count in the forty-ounce total. If you are eating lots of fruits and vegetables, you may need less than my recommendation.

Unintentional dehydration adds significantly to pain and suffering. If you get a stomach ache or a headache, try a glass of water first. Give some time for it to work its magic before popping an aspirin. It will surprise you when you feel the benefit.

Take water several minutes before you eat each meal and an hour after. Finally, remember that if you feel thirsty, you are already dehydrated. The key understanding is: when body fluids decrease, so too does energy.

Think about What You Eat

Eat a green salad, going easy on the salad dressing if it is mayonnaise-based. Try putting fresh lemon juice and extra virgin olive oil on it with just a touch of salt. When you eat, stay alert to how your body reacts to what you feed it. Eat as much raw food as possible. Go slow with the food changes, a little at a time, but be consistent. Become an expert at sensing the energy, or lack of it, that you feel.

When you get lots of burps and churning, rethink your menus and remove the food that isn't really agreeing with your metabolism and body type; it is draining precious energy, especially if it is highly processed. Eat lots of fruit on an empty stomach, and then eat the rest of your meal. Identify foods that stay with you and provide long lasting energy. All of this, seemingly unimportant, will assist healing as it increases endurance.

Take a Break

Try a mid-afternoon stress break. Over fifty years ago, an old physiologist once told me that when taking a break, "Never stand when you can sit, never sit when you can lie down, and never lie down when you can lie down and put your feet up." Be sure to elevate your feet when you take your twenty-minute break. Also, close your eyes, as they take in so much data and tend to stimulate body processes. (Of course, the eyes can also be used in examining a relaxing scene.) See what pops into your thoughts or alters your perspective. Planned distress release reduces the possibility of compromising the immune system and getting infections. This quiet time, continued long after grief has lessened, will add years to your life.

Don't immediately expect yourself to have the same quality of output you had before your loss. Mistakes, confusion, and disorganization are the norm. Accept them and don't condemn yourself.

39. Start Each Day with a Strong Affirmative Action

Each day when you get out of bed and you are hit with the reality of your loss, have a way to counter the grief assault. Say out loud (or silently, if you prefer): "I am adapting" or "I am capable of bearing this burden." I know a man who starts every day with, "Thank you for the light" as soon as his feet hit the floor. Print out a statement that you will press on and put it in a spot where you see it upon rising. Try "I will meet the challenge of this day." Or have an inspiring thought taped to your bedpost or mirror that you read as you climb out of bed or go into the bathroom, such as "Today I will use the wisdom within my heart." Ask your higher power to help you follow through. Recognize that when we grieve, our higher thoughts are not always easy to come by. Each day, ask for the wisdom to make healthy choices. How you start each day is crucial to how the day progresses.

If you have a picture of your loved one on your night stand or dresser, and you awake to see his or her face staring at you, stop and think. Does seeing this picture cause great pain when you start the day? Does it bring a rush of emptiness and sadness? If so, remove and place the picture in another section of your home or room to reduce the shock when you awaken. Later, as healing progresses, you can return it to its original position.

....

40. Test Your Guilt and Let It Go

....

Although not everyone who is mourning experiences guilt, it is a fairly common experience. *It is nearly impossible to love someone, suffer the death of the person, and later not feel guilty about something in the relationship.* It's so easy to lay an unnecessary guilt trip on ourselves. And often, previous unresolved guilt feelings from childhood may add to the present guilt.

For our purposes we will deal with two types of guilt: true cause-and-effect guilt (you did something you shouldn't have done and feel bad about it) and neurotic guilt (there is nothing you could have done at the time, but now you are convinced there was). Most, if not all, guilt associated with the death of a loved one is neurotic in nature. That is, the feelings of guilt are way out of proportion to the cause; it is not true cause-and-effect guilt.

I have heard many guilt-ridden mourners say, "I should have taken him to a different emergency room," "I should have gotten him to stop smoking or drinking," "I should have taken him to the hospital sooner, even though he didn't want to go," "What she said to me went right over my head," or "I didn't think the illness was that serious." These all reinforce unnecessary guilt.

Guilt surfaces in many other forms as well. There are numerous supposed failures in relationships that result in neurotic guilt feelings—not being present at certain times, especially at the moment of death, feeling relief after the death, thinking you are not feeling bad enough, not intervening in a stronger way when hospital care seems inadequate, feeling one should have visited more frequently, not doing what the other wanted to do in earlier years, thinking "why was I spared and she had to die," and the list can go on and on. It may be helpful to remember that there is relatively little in the world that we can actually control.

Never forget: we all review our relationship with our loved one, and if we had a chance to do it over, would quickly change some of the things we did or did not do. That is part of the human condition. And most of us are into this kind of self-deprecating thinking after a loved one dies. I felt guilty when my mother died because I could not remember the last time I had said to her "I love you." A psychologist saved the day and shocked me to my senses by posing one question to me: "Lou, don't you think your mother knew you loved her?"

The point is, you need to consider whether or not you are second-guessing yourself, now that you look back and see the alternative. You did what you felt you had to do at the time, given the pressures and circumstances. Test your guilt.

Evaluate your behavior with these two words: "intent" and "deliberate." With most all of the guilt generated when mourning, you did not deliberately intend to set out to inflict pain or suffering or contribute to the circumstances surrounding the death. Few people do. As you look back now with hindsight, it is easy to latch onto another approach as the cure-all. Repeatedly tell yourself that you are not all-knowing: you could not realize all of the possible scenarios that might evolve. No one can.

If by some outside chance it is true guilt, then seek forgiveness—and you can talk to your deceased loved one and say you are sorry and ask to be forgiven. Most important: there is extremely effective medicine for true cause-and-effect guilt—self-forgiveness. It never fails, and without it you cannot grow, work through, or adapt to your loss. So stop punishing yourself; it will not bring back your loved one. Make a decision to deal with your guilt, as it will not go away until you do.

Be careful not to mix shame with guilt. Sometimes mourners are ashamed with the way they have responded to a crisis or by the stigma associated with the type of death (suicide, alcoholism, etc.). That shame means you feel you are a bad person because of your response or due to the nature of the situation. Again, it is totally unrealistic, and you will only be increasing anxiety through detachment. Guilt, whether neurotic or real, usually has to do with your perceived behavior or a lack of it. Be sure you are focusing on what you supposedly did or did not do, and not on indicting yourself. Your self-talk is crucial in this regard. Tell yourself you did the best you could at the time and dispel all self-limiting messages. Toss out talking to yourself or others with guilt language—"I should have" or "I could have"—and you will pull yourself out of the guilt pit.

Also, ask yourself if you have any remnants of guilt from your childhood that may add to the guilt you are presently dealing with. Are you following a childhood script of pleasing everyone or trying to be perfect? Discuss this possibility with a professional, should it exist, so that you can then deal with your loss.

41. Let Go of "If Onlys," "What Ifs," and "Shoulds"

A woman whose husband had died after a short stay in the hospital said to me, "If only he had called out sooner that he wasn't feeling well, I could have gotten help sooner." A widower said, "If only I had gone down to the seashore more with her." A mother whose son died in a one-car accident observed, "If only he had not taken the car to school that day." All were looking back and second-guessing. Many survivors have said, "What if my doctor had been at the hospital at the time of the emergency? I bet Jon would have received exactly what he needed and would not have suffered as much as he did."

Eliminate doubt by examining one question: did I do what I thought I should do at the time? Of course, you did. Yes, you were under pressure. But you had no intention of doing something that in the long run could have hurt your loved one. If you had the power to prevent the outcome, you would have exercised it. You didn't. No one does. Let go of the critical stance you are taking toward yourself.

There's a big difference between regret and guilt. It's okay to regret you or your loved one not making a different choice; regret does *not* imply personal responsibility. But do not lay a disguised guilt trip on yourself. True cause-and-effect guilt means personal responsibility. "If onlys" and "What ifs" *never* fall into that category, but they can lead to anger and much anxiety. We have to let go of anything that is not serving us.

All of the above hindsight is often followed by friends or family members who give unsolicited advice beginning with "You should." You should go back to school or work or get on with your life. You should not be looking for companionship (if widowed). You should be getting back to normal by now. You should not be doing what you are doing because others will think you are "losing it." Forget the word "should" and make choices based on what you believe is right for you at this point in your life. Let the normal change of you occur under your direction.

42. Use a Transitional Object or Symbol for Comfort

A transitional object is anything that represents a positive emotional or symbolic connection between the mourner and the deceased loved one. It can be something the deceased owned, used, or wore, or something that was given to the mourner. It could be something in nature that is full of symbolic meaning or spiritual sustenance that the deceased liked. It could be an event that occurred at an opportune time. A strong transitional object could be a collage of pictures that represent experiences or memories that bring comforting reminders.

Here is what Kathy Love, a colleague of mine, said about transitional objects after her mother and father died within months of each other:

> Hold on to treasured items and collect new ones. My sister, brother, and I took small kitchen items that held memories for us. They were priceless to us. While I was going through my parents' clothing, I nabbed some and had a friend make a quilt for all three of us. My parent's picture was placed in the middle of it…just beautiful and appreciated. If I learned anything from all of this, it is this: You can't appreciate a rainbow until you have seen the rain. Sounds hokey, but you sure can appreciate the little things more when things were really tough for a while.

Symbols are often variable keepsakes that represent something other for the mourner than just their physical appearance. These objects (flowers, butterflies, rainbows, birds, etc.) can be major symbols of that powerful elusive thing called hope, which is a massive force in coping with loss and fully reentering life. They often give encouragement, inspiration, and constant reminding in the process of adapting because they are part of our spiritual life. These symbols can also be experiences or characteristics of your loved one that you see in your children or other persons.

If any object, picture, or memento that you look at brings added sadness, then put it away or get rid of it. You may at a later time be able to look at it in a different light. If not, you will eventually know for sure that it is better to no longer keep it.

Here is another example of a transitional symbol in the form of a penny (the keepsake object) that came years later, as told in the following true story related to me by Marilyn Zimmerman, who lives in North Carolina. Her son had just graduated from the State Police Academy in Ohio when he was killed by a drunk driver. She had a number of unusual experiences, and several years later was helping other bereaved parents, when the following occurred:

On Thursday morning, January 11, 2007, I had an unusual after-death experience or sign. Two days prior, on the ninth of January, we, my husband and I, met with a lady who had lost her nineteen-year-old son, Brian, in a freak accident in which he was struck by lightning and died three weeks later. We talked for over two hours and told her many of the stories about our after-death experiences, many of which included finding pennies after mentioning our son, Eric, or thinking about him.

My husband and I had been talking about the Tuesday meeting on Wednesday evening, before we went to bed. As I lay in bed that night I was feeling very sad. I felt the pain of another mother having to lose her son and cried for her and her son, Brian, and my Eric. I said my prayers and asked for Brian and Eric to give us some signs. I prayed for my mom and dad and all of my passed relatives, my spirit guides and angels, to help us get some signs from them. I finally fell to sleep.

At 2:30 a.m. I woke up to go to the bathroom (as usual) and then again at 4:28. This time I walked into the dark bathroom, did not turn on the lights, and started to sit down. As I was just sitting down something hit my right shoulder and hit the floor. I felt it, then heard it. I couldn't see anything. At first I was scared, not being awake at all. I sat down and popped right back up and turned the light on real quick. I looked down and there was a penny lying on the right side of the toilet on the floor. I bent over and picked it up, and said "Thank you," cried a little, and woke up my husband, Fred, right away. I verbally repeated the exact experience with the penny in my hand and we were both assured, once again, that these events are purposeful, spontaneous, and meant to give comfort, even though there is no earthly explanation of how this could possibly happen.

Transitional objects like the penny, a blanket, or food can become part of the continuing new relationship to the deceased, immeasurable aids in adapting to the new environment without the physical presence of the loved one. Hold the object in your hands in a quiet setting, look at it, and see what memories pop into your thoughts.

43. Don't Set Timelines for Mourning

Those in mourning often ask the question, "When will all this end?" The answer is, no one knows. There are a multitude of factors that shape the length of time deep mourning persists. The cause of death, age, role, rituals, relationship, previous losses, unfinished business, and how you have coped in the past will play a role. Assumptions, beliefs, and the perception of isolation will also be involved. These and other variables (like insecurity and resistance to, instead of acceptance of, the unknowable) can shorten or lengthen the grief process and how you adapt to a world without your loved one.

The point of importance here is that you do not base your grieving on someone else's agenda or your preconceived notion of how long it took someone else to deal with a similar loss. Your relationship with the deceased has no duplicate and neither does your grief. *Grieve according to your pace.*

On the other hand, when grief goes on indefinitely, or you feel you are grieving more intensely than you should with your present loss, it may be there are other unresolved losses that you never fully dealt with. These losses could have occurred earlier in life or more recently and, for whatever reason, you pushed them away and tried to forget them. It is quite normal for earlier losses to resurface and be a part of your present grief response. And these losses do not necessarily have to be a death-related loss. Here is where a grief counselor can be of assistance in helping you deal with one loss at a time and understanding your intense grief.

44. Review the Relationship with Your Deceased Loved One

Although you will be thinking much about your loved one in the context of the loss of his or her immediate presence, taking time to review the entire relationship will be a significant tool for coping. It will be most helpful if you can do the review after the most intense part of grieving has begun to abate. The process of starting from the beginning and going through the years at first may bring more tears, some heartfelt thanks, and unpleasant events that should remain in the past. Your review can also help you highlight specific loving memories that, through the months and years to come, will bring much comfort.

One of the ways to love in separation and establish a new relationship with the deceased is to pick out some of the characteristics of your loved one or the ways he or she helped you realize a particular goal. Model his or her giving. Focus on the good qualities and use them, even further develop them, with the intention of honoring the deceased.

Make a List of Good Thoughts

Not surprisingly, as you go back through the years, some memories will bring up many forgotten events. This is a healthy and normal part of your grief work, as it will allow you to identify thoughts and feelings you may need to discuss and grieve with someone you trust. All relationships have happy and unhappy times. Jot down the good thoughts so you can use them when you dwell too long on your sadness. Take out your list and think of how you feel as you pore over the good thoughts associated with your loved one. Build on your list for several days. Perhaps some emotions that surface will have never been previously worked through.

However, in order to release pain and establish the new relationship—so that you can reinvest in life—conflicting thoughts and feelings need to be resolved. The process of review is not a one-day event; it is ongoing over time, and gradually you will be able to withdraw some of the great emotional investment you had in the loved one. You will replace it with emotion that recognizes the physical absence of your loved one, but also with one that forever has a place deep in your heart.

....

In summary, do three things:

▸ Find a quiet place where you can be alone, and start your review from the beginning.
▸ Identify the good and the bad so that you have a realistic view of the relationship, not an idealized one. Use the good to form lasting memories.
▸ Grieve what you feel you need to, and find assistance, either from a trusted friend or a professional, if you discover events or feelings that are bothersome.

....

45. Never Blame or Complain

Blaming and complaining are easy traps to fall into when defenses are low and you are mourning the death of a loved one. They are often a form of excuse-making for not doing what needs to be done. Whiny complaints frequently show up when mourners are deeply distressed or at their wits' end. Once again, like so many other negatives that surface during grief work, these two saboteurs take away from charting the course back to wholeness. They muddy your thinking waters just as they remove energy from your daily allotment. In fact, blame and complaints are another form of negative thinking and a proven downer for brain maintenance.

Blaming and complaining are quick routes to seeing yourself as a victim. And you know self-victimization immediately reduces your personal power to take control of your grief work. You are putting yourself out of the recovery network and your physical self in jeopardy. These two negatives will also wreck your relationship with good listeners you rely on.

You only have so much energy, and when you start running on empty, it affects the way you think and relate to anyone in your nurturing community. More importantly, ask yourself if you are shifting responsibility, creating scapegoats when assuming more responsibility for the course of your grief work is the way to go.

Assess how much you engage in blaming and complaining thoughts on a given day, and realize you are canceling out whatever positive energy you previously generated. We *create* what we experience. Set a goal that you will not blame or complain for one day. Then work toward two, three, and more days until you have changed this aspect of your thought-life.

Assert yourself. Make your needs clear but do your part. In the final analysis, only your decisions and behavioral changes will lead to healing. Refuse to take the focus off your actions and put it on the actions or inaction of others. It's what you do that really counts.

46. Solicit Honest Feedback

Be radically honest with your feelings, and ask your friends to be honest with you—and with the answers they give to questions you may ask. Telling the truth about how you really feel often leads to more trusting relationships. Speak with integrity. For many, this is not easy to do. In addition, it takes courage to ask friends what they really think about how you are responding to life without your loved one. Yet it can be one of the most productive actions to take to help evaluate where you have been and what direction you may need to go.

Asking others simple questions such as, "What do you think about _____?" "What is your opinion?" "How would you react?" gives you information to analyze and include in your deliberations before taking action. There is no obligation to take their advice.

Of course, the key consideration in soliciting feedback is the sources you pick. And while you obviously want to find people who are trusting, wise, nonjudgmental, and loving, in certain circumstances those you are not close to, even strangers, can give some amazing insights into coping with change. In your discussion, simply ask, "What would you do if you were in my shoes?" How you phrase your inquiry and the timing is what needs to be thought out. There are innumerable ways of looking at how to adapt to life problems, and the insights that come from your inquiries will provide a whole new set of choices to consider. This approach can help you to become stronger, wiser, and better able to adapt to the new circumstances of your life.

47. Accept the "Year of the Firsts"

One of your best routes to accommodating the reality of your loss is being aware of and accepting all the "firsts" that occur without your loved one. The "year of the firsts" refers to all of the many times in which you will be doing things that normally would include your loved one and, for the first time, he or she is not there. It could be the first time you go on vacation or to visit relatives, eat at a familiar restaurant, go to church, attend a wedding, go to the beach, meet old friends, see a movie—anything can point out the absence. It is a jolt, an expected time of sadness.

What can you do? Initially, just being aware that these events will commonly take place is useful. You may need someone to be with so that you can talk about what it all means. It may easily bring forth tears and much heartache. Tell yourself it is perfectly normal to feel this way. That's the way memory works.

Be prepared for a grief response on certain anniversaries, holidays, birthdays, and other family events. (See **#49, Make a Plan to Deal with Holidays, Anniversaries, and other Special Days**.) Again, don't suppress your feelings. Seek ways to let them out—write, walk, talk, tell yourself this is part of adapting, and do whatever you need to do with the intention of reducing the distress of the moment. Say, "I am doing this to gradually release the buildup of painful feelings."

FIVE

Powerful Long-Term Healing Strategies

You cannot always control what goes on outside. But you can always control what goes on inside.

—DR. WAYNE DYER

Up to now we've looked at how successful mourners develop their inner lives, continually make adjustments to deal with the new scenes that must be faced, become determined to take action, build a nurturing support network, and learn to love in separation. Now let's look at some additional strategies that can be used for the rest of your life in dealing with your present loss, the challenges yet to come, and the future losses that predictably occur as we age.

48. Use Color to Influence and Inspire

Little things can make a big difference in how you feel. In particular, colors influence mood, emotion, spirituality, attitude, and behavior. They can also influence energy levels. Bright colors can be a pick-me-up at certain times. For now, stay away from purple and black, as they tend to add to your down moods. Pink (for love), orange, red—sometimes referred to as an emotional color—and yellows (for confidence) have a positive effect on mood.

Green and blue are soothing and relaxing, and promote healing. Buy a few additional green plants to place in the most lived-in areas of your house or apartment; they are alive and flourishing and can have much symbolic meaning. They also emit oxygen and absorb carbon dioxide, which contributes to a healthier atmosphere. Consider buying and caring for goldfish. Again, they are alive and colorful and can reduce the sense of isolation.

Compare the clothing you presently wear and what you wore in the past that made you feel good. If necessary, purchase a new outfit or two. Try different color combinations and consider the way they affect you. Red can be bold and inspiring. Consider wearing white, an energizer and a sign of purity and kindness, as part of an outfit with the intention of making a new beginning in life. Pairing intention with color choice is essential for best results. Make a commitment on a specific day to lift your mood by wearing bright colors of your taste.

Also, consider upgrading the colors in your workspace or in your special room at home. Is there anything you can do, short of a paint job, to brighten up your surroundings? Incidentally, I know a number of mourners who have had a room redone in their home or have painted one themselves. Even consider changing the color on your computer screen for a few months, or purchase a bright new screen saver.

Experiment with colors that could be most useful to your imaginative faculty. In a quiet setting, close your eyes and visualize a particular color within and around you. Note the effects it has on you physically and/or emotionally. Take your time with this experience and take notes on what surfaces from within. Then make use of that color best suited for the needs you wish to meet.

Adding stimulation to the environment you walk into by way of brightness, and dispatching darkness, can be another way to reinvest in your new life. Science has made it clear that light affects mood in a positive way. Or you may need relaxing colors in a special place in your home. Try various combinations to suit your tastes and the mood you wish to create.

49. Make a Plan to Deal with Holidays, Anniversaries, and Other Special Days

The emphasis here is on planning. Holidays after the death of a loved one can be especially difficult to move through, as well as a variety of anniversary dates. If the loss has occurred close to big holidays, say within four months or less, or on an anniversary or birthday, you may still be experiencing some degree of shock, numbness, and disbelief. If that is the case, the effect of these significant dates may be mitigated. The following year, however, after the shock and numbness have worn off, the dates may be far more difficult for you.

This can be especially disconcerting since the belief is that the second year gets easier when it is, in fact, sometimes—I repeat, sometimes—more difficult. You may feel you are not doing as well as expected, and this can be discouraging. But be aware that although the second year may be more painful than the first, your reaction is normal given the timeline.

Assert Yourself

Anticipating the pain and loneliness to be faced, as well as what to say to friends and family, is often worse than the unfolding of the particular day. Yet Christmas, Hanukkah, Thanksgiving, anniversaries, birthdays, reunions—the first anything without the loved one—are often made even worse when mourners do not assert themselves about what they can and cannot do when it involves family. Keep a journal of your grief around these special times as another outlet for feelings. Here are several additional considerations to facilitate honoring your loved one and yourself on these special days:

- As a primary mourner, *your needs come first*, and you have to gently make them known to all concerned. Tell family and friends specifically what you can and cannot do. Do this at various times and in appropriate places, even in your home well before the holiday. Explain what you feel and how you wish to observe the day. Discuss what can be added or deleted from the usual celebration and what you would find most difficult to deal with. Emphasize that you have just so much emotional energy, and say no when necessary.

- If the event was normally held at your home, you may want to eat out, have someone else hold it this year, or have others assume more responsibility, to take the load off your shoulders. It's okay and necessary to say no to your old commitments when you know it will be too much for you. As your grief changes over time, you can assume old responsibilities or make further deletions or additions, if you feel like it.

- You don't have to follow the exact schedule or routines of the past. Traditions can change, even if they are many years old. Consider starting a new tradition. Whatever you feel will be the most difficult part of the holiday for you can be altered, held at a different time, or left out for this year. Let whatever you feel will reduce unnecessary stress and sadness be your guide. It is easier to prevent distress than it is to cope with it once it builds and takes hold of the body. Anything left out of one year can always be brought back the next, if you are ready for it.

- There is nothing wrong with reducing the time you spend at events or in preparation for the day. You may not want to send cards or buy gifts. You might wish the day wouldn't come. Regardless of what others do in your family, before each holiday or celebration, tell all concerned what your level of participation will be. You alone know what your energy level is like and what your resources can take without undue strain. Feel free to say you will leave early, not participate in one or more aspects of the celebration, step outside if you feel especially sad, or come later to the event.

- Find a way to symbolically honor your deceased loved one. You may want to take a day off from work. Make it a habit to acknowledge the memory of your loved one at major family events. You or someone in the family can make a toast to the loved one, display a picture or photo album, have the deceased's favorite dessert or meal, say a prayer, display or give something he or she created, place a flower in a special place at the table, or leave one space at the table empty (have everyone sit in different places). And it's okay if tears flow; it is a common and normal response.

- Tell yourself and accept the fact that the holiday will be different. Identify what emotions you are feeling and express them to your grief companion. Your goal is to make the best of it by dealing with the emotions you are experiencing. You may have to telephone friends or family members. Don't set yourself up for additional pain by expecting there will be only sorrow, or the whole scene will be nothing but a major source of distress.

- Diligently manage your anticipation. Keep things simple and focus on the values, beliefs, joy, and wisdom of the deceased. At the appropriate holiday, give yourself a present from your loved one, and remember that laughter and a smile are still important parts of life. Last but not least, be sure to include your walking program on that particular day and allow yourself to cry as you walk, if you feel like it.

MY HOLIDAY PLAN

Finally, here are ten statements to help you develop a plan for holidays and celebrations. Advanced planning is essential. Fill in each open space. Write as much as you need to.

1. I anticipate the most difficult part of the coming holiday will be _____.

2. The people I feel will be sources of anxiety for me are _____.

3. What will help me most to get through the coming holiday is _____.

4. The people I believe will be the most helpful to me are _____.

5. The most comfortable conversations for me will center on _____.

6. I will celebrate the memory of my loved one on this holiday by _____.

7. I will express my needs to family/friends by saying _____.

8. I will reduce my participation in the festivities by _____.

9. In order to accomplish my plan, the first thing I will do is _____.

10. I will walk for _____ minutes each day.

In summary, advance planning is a must. This also applies to the monthly anniversaries of the death early in your grief, if they are difficult to confront. With the help and cooperation of all, you, your family, and friends can make it through the special days and celebrate a life that has been lived. However, make every effort to structure the day, not isolate yourself, and make your needs known; it all begins with you.

50. Identify Your Fears and Confront Them

At various times in life, we all have to deal with fear. In fact, a considerable amount of life is fear-driven. When real danger is present, fear is a natural protective response. When you are grieving, fear is a common source of unnecessary suffering because it is an unnatural, highly distorted negative thought. Along with worry, it is mostly generated by thinking of the future without your loved one and a sense of loss of control.

More specifically, our fears may include financial problems, feelings of abandonment or rejection, poor self-esteem, assuming new responsibilities, thinking the loved one will be forgotten—the list goes on and on. Preoccupation with the future is fueled by the absence of our loved one and can be managed by staying focused on the present moment and doing our best on this particular day.

Your innate abilities, and we all have them, are more powerful than any fear you may have to confront in adapting to the unfamiliar. Begin by identifying and describing the specific cause of your feelings. Then you can start the task of dealing with it.

Everybody Freaks Out

Worry and fear are cellmates, and both are normal human responses to severe stress. Almost all fears are learned. This is significant to dwell on, because if we learn our fears, we can persist and unlearn them. Actor Hill Harper's definition of fear is "False Evidence Appearing Real." Fear of the future without your loved one is a false fear based on your habituated belief that you don't have the courage and strength to adapt. It is normal to feel this way at this time. The uncontrolled imagination fuels that fear. Refuse to allow fear to be the roadblock to the wisdom that lies within.

The key question is: how do you cope with your fear, whatever it may be?

There is no magic formula for banishing fear. But it can be lessened and often eliminated over time. There is nothing that overpowers fear more completely than love; it is our greatest defense. That is why our friends are so important in sharing fears. Here are proven ways, used by many, to manage fear and reduce the emotional and physical effects of this common emotion when grieving.

The most important first step is *acknowledgment of fear, coupled with the strong commitment to manage it*. Concealment is common, especially if you are a male. Admitting your fears to yourself, and especially to a trusted friend, is absolutely essential to the formation of any plan to deal with them. Put your fear in writing, examine it carefully, and think about potential solutions before talking to your friend.

The more you keep fear hidden the more you isolate yourself from support and your own defenses to deal with it. It would be especially helpful if you could find someone who is dealing with or has dealt with a similar fear in order to consider strategies.

Commitment begins with the intention of reversing the language of fear. The use of language in describing fear is powerful because self-talk plays a major role in what you experience and in reducing anxiety. Since fear is learned, it is created by what you think and observe, and how you feed these thoughts; it especially affects your decision-making.

In addition, that same inner monologue has a gigantic influence on behavior. Don't imprison yourself. Never use "I am," as in "I am fearful," when describing your fear. Use "I frequently experience" instead. Distance yourself from fear; refuse to make it your soul-mate when you describe it. Tell yourself "I am capable of conquering fear." "I am not this fear." Do not believe you are what you feel. Develop and repeat your own positive affirmations. These will strengthen the quality of your internal monologue, which is always with you. The key is to use them every day, whether you are having a good day or a bad one.

Analyze and seek information about the source of fear. Search for the gift behind the fear. What is your fear asking? What do you need? Do you fear not being loved? Why are you afraid you won't be able to reinvest in life? Why are you afraid you won't be able to live by yourself? Search for the experiences in life that have created the beliefs behind your fears. Where do they come from and who influenced you? Was it a traumatic event or essentially self-created by negative thinking or poor role models?

Strengthen your inner life to reshape the beliefs and fearful thoughts and you can create a new reality. This may mean seeing a counselor or talking with a dear friend to sort it out.

Take small steps. Ponder. Contemplate. What is the fantasized worst-case scenario? Once you answer that question, you can now decide on what your real fear might be. What are you telling yourself about the object of fear? That you can't deal with it? That it has more power than you? Not so!

Challenge fearful thoughts. They are essentially limiting beliefs, allowing fear to grow and dominate your thought life. Locate the origin of these thoughts, then change them. You need counter-thoughts. Convince yourself that you are more resourceful and powerful today than any fear.

All of the experts on fear say with one voice: repeatedly face your fears and move through them. Fear gets power when you back off. You can be afraid and still push through the fearful circumstances. Play whatever mind-game is necessary. Practice in your mind's eye what you will do when you are confronted. What will you say to yourself, and most important, what action will you take?

Turn to your higher power and your faith for assistance. This is a powerful but seldom recommended resource. Ask for strength the moment you sense fear is making inroads on your thinking. Ask for the wisdom to deal with it.

So what is the bottom line in dealing with fear? Break the *habit of fear*. Accept it as false evidence. Make a fierce commitment to confront it. Change the way you talk to yourself and think about fear. Get information on its source to enable you to alter your beliefs and challenge the false face of fear. Use self-coaching in the repetitive use of affirmations and calling on your faith.

And then, the action step: the willingness to feel the fear and do the thing you fear.

Worry and fear are demanding partners—but both are controlled by one characteristic we all possess: courage. That is what each of us has to muster when facing fear and doing what we know deep inside just has to be done.

51. Make New Friends Continually— for the Rest of Your Life

As mentioned in chapter 4, a grief companion is an absolute must. However, the next level of personal strength and fulfillment evolves through developing social bonds to find a sense of importance and reduce isolation. Everyone needs to be a part of something greater than the self; we all have a deep need to be loved and belong. While this need can be met in many ways, it is most obvious in our circle of friendships and developing a strong social support network for life. Centuries ago, Aelred of Rievaulx, an abbot, homilist, and historian, wrote, "The best medicine in life is a friend." Social scientists tell us that a strong social circle clearly extends the lifespan, tends to make us healthier, and reduces the negative effects of stress. We are social beings who thrive on inter-action with others.

You can easily increase friendships in three ways: (1) reciprocate the caring you receive, (2) join groups where you meet new people, and (3) transition from acquaintances to friendships. This means that in reaching out you need to carefully risk some self-disclosure and see how an acquaintance responds. Yes, you risk rejection, but gradual self-disclosure over time is the initial building block in strong friendships. Patience, respect, loyalty, trust, and similar values are all part of the mix.

Because interpersonal relationships are so important to physi-cal and mental health, adopt the frame of mind that you will add to your friendship pool until the day you die. Interpersonal competence is as important as a healthy heart. Become aware of the role of sensitivity to interpersonal needs, honesty, and humil-ity in establishing connections with anyone. Conversations with faithful friends continually present new options for nourishing relationships by the manner in which you address and relate to the person. Regular communication is a part of good friendship and good grief work. See **#100, Develop Your Social Skills**.

Opportunities to make new friends will frequently present themselves. Whether at work, play, vacation, shopping, or virtu-ally anywhere people gather, the possibility of striking up a friend-ship presents itself. Find people with similar goals who aren't judgmental or critical.

It takes time to develop trusting relationships, and you need to give a big part of yourself to the task. Be assured, the dividends will be amazing, for your general life as well as whenever grief revisits. The first and important step is the *intention* to look for new friends who share your interests and values. Initially, it is more important to find people who are willing to listen to you and validate your grief. Later, as you feel stronger and less vulnerable, you can be the good listener. Then commit to *listening more than you speak* as you learn to put yourself in their shoes and open your heart to new friendships.

Remember as well to make specific time to improve relationships with other family members and friends as the months go by after the death of your loved one. These connections will provide a big boost to how you feel physically and to how you heal emotionally. Try working toward a large and diverse network. Many psychiatrists emphasize that the quality of our interpersonal relationships is as important as the food we eat or the vitamins we take.

Why Other People Are a Source of Joy and Happiness

Friendships are among the most potent sources of hope. And hope is not some will-of-the-wisp factor. Healthy friendships make us feel important and accepted—a lifelong need—and a major way to cultivate and nourish hope. Close friends motivate and strengthen our belief that we can achieve and develop strategies to reinvest in life. That is a centerpiece of hope. Put another way, happiness is doing, not getting.

In contrast, keep in mind the negative effects of isolation on hope. Science has proven that such effects lead to ill health. Whatever you do, don't let your social structure decay. Not only does that lead to increased isolation and frequently the depression that comes with it, but you will be losing out on one of the most powerful ongoing healers in life. Those around us influence our healing. When you isolate yourself, little happens and time moves more slowly.

Keep in mind, it is not unusual for a friend or two to abandon you after the death of your loved one, sometimes as a result of not knowing how to offer ongoing support, sometimes because you are not following their agenda for healing. This is another reason to find other people whom you value and with whom you connect.

BREAKING THE ISOLATION BARRIER

- Accept invitations for dinner at your neighbor's home, even if you don't feel like going. Or accompany a friend who invites you to go shopping. This will necessitate talking and reaching out. Decide that you will make the first move and create a rule that you will talk to at least three other people every day, especially if you live alone.

- Choose to join a social group that meets weekly. Look on bulletin boards and the Internet. There are many groups with a variety of interests from bridge and book clubs to line-dancing, golf, and bowling leagues. Look for something in your local newspaper that seems interesting to you, or join your local gym. Don't be afraid to try something you know little about.

▸ Others you do not consider close friends, as often happens, may turn out to be most sensitive to your needs. Look for those who have common interests and values or call someone you have lost touch with. Evaluate who fits into this category and make every effort to cultivate their friendship.

▸ Make it a rule that you will not stay by yourself all day in your home or apartment. Decide the night before where you will go the following day so that you will be around people and have to talk to them. One widow said that 5:00 p.m. was the most difficult time for her to be alone. Each day she planned an activity that took her out of the house at that hour.

▸ Last and most important, when friends don't quite live up to your expectations, be willing to cut them some slack. Occasional disagreements are bound to occur. We all have boundaries that have to be observed, yet we all have our imperfections to be tolerated. Be willing to give a sincere apology if you are at fault.

52. Join a Support Group

Don't shy away from this possibility, especially if you are a male. Sometimes your family and friends are unable to provide the assistance you need, especially for a long period of time. Therefore, look for a grief support group at your local hospice, hospital, or church. If you are mourning the death of a child, consider Compassionate Friends or one of the Healing Hearts groups that have been started in some communities by bereaved parents. It will make it easier to deal with stress, and you will be less apt to come down with a stress-related illness. The healing power of these communities is well-known and has long been demonstrated.

Finding a support group may be especially necessary when some of your support persons start to think you should be "getting over it" and begin to abandon you. This is not an uncommon occurrence. Education about the normalcy of your longer-than-expected experience can be an important outcome of any group.

Everyone's grief is one of a kind. You can learn much about grief and grief work in the group, and often you may be able to connect with another who is going through a similar loss. Helping each other in the listening process—an act of love—is usually a healing experience for both. As a widow recently told me, "Your problem doesn't seem as bad when you hear of others who have similar problems just like yours."

Support groups reduce the sense of isolation, become networks for cultivating new friends who understand what you are going through, and provide a place where you can really tell it like it is without embarrassing anyone. As with going to a doctor or a lawyer, you have to find the right group. If you don't connect with the group leader, then look for another group.

You may be thinking that a support group is not for you, but give it a try, especially if you feel it is a sign of weakness to look for help. There is a palpable energy that is generated in these groups which has motivated participants to change their expectations of what they are capable of accomplishing. I have seen many new friendships emerge that are extremely helpful in meeting the new challenges imposed by a loved one's death. Simply being in a supportive, caring environment is conducive to saying what you really feel and might otherwise hold in.

You will get new ideas from others in the group; there will be someone to call in the evening, and you will always have a place to go early in your grief where you can say exactly how you feel. You will not have to pretend you are feeling okay about your loss to please someone. The grief process varies immensely among individuals, and there is so much to share with group members and, of course, learn from the facilitator. As many grief group members have said, "You know you are not alone."

53. Work on Your Patience

Grief work takes time, not the two or three weeks that employers and some relatives seem to expect. You cannot rush your mourning; each of us has our own pace. Become familiar with what you require, and don't feel self-conscious if you are not responding like someone else in your immediate family. Although it takes a great deal of time to adapt to big life changes, we live in and have been conditioned by a society that expects immediate results. Grief and healing hurry for no one.

Your patience is an expression of great wisdom in dealing with uncertainty; it will build a strong inner life and your eventual healing will be solid. Program yourself to accept each day as it comes, knowing you are capable and will get through it. Go easy on those who do not understand what you are going through.

People Say Dumb Things

Your patience will be especially tested when people say the wrong thing at the wrong time. There are many of those folks out there. When people suggest at the funeral or memorial service that you will find someone else, it was God's will, or you still have your other children, or give you all kinds of advice without being asked, you may want to lash out in anger. Save your energy and time. It only weakens you. Let the anger go, for your sake. That is wisdom in action. These people mean well, but are commonly ignorant of your real needs and the grief process. Many are full of death anxiety (a conditioned fear of death), and need to say something. Your patience is an integral part of understanding their deficiency and reducing your own stress.

As many mourners do, pray for patience to accept whatever comes that you are unable to prevent from occurring. Be patient with the painful emotions that show up. Remind yourself that you do *not* have control over what people say, but you have total control over how you will react and how you will mourn each day. Do not worry about tomorrow. Muster your patience for the next hour, or maybe even the next minute, but do not try to focus too much on the rest of the day.

54. When You Have a Bad Day, Make Contact

When you have a bad day—where your thoughts are filled with deep sadness and remorse more than usual—recognize that it is part of the healing process; such days will come and, most assuredly, they will go. But they will test your inner strength and mold you. Acknowledge and accept them as a normal part of the work of grief. You can help yourself by not giving in or withdrawing. Here are suggestions for dealing with it:

- Don't sit there and feel miserable all day. Now more than ever, if you want to manage your pain, you need to connect, make contact. Call someone you trust and explain what is happening. See if he or she can meet you for coffee or lunch. Or invite the person over to the house. Avoid contacts with people you feel may not understand or will drag you down even further.
- Put off a difficult chore that will only add more stress to your day.

- Look for something that will distract you from the thoughts that are dragging you down. Consider going someplace you don't normally frequent: the zoo, the racetrack, the art museum. You will at least be around people.
- Lovingly share something you have been given. It can refocus your inner thoughts.
- Flash back and direct all of your attention on when you have been okay—when you have had good days—and even before your loved one died. Think about what you did or did not do.

Expect bad days; everyone has them. The only thing that can easily limit your progress is the failure to accept the temporary regression and renew your determination after a bad day. Grief is not a smooth, consistent upward climb; it runs into reversals, ups, and downs like a roller coaster, and you feel you have lost headway. Never allow your imagination to work in reverse and pummel your mind with all the old defeating phrases and pictures of futility.

Bad days provide another opportunity to choose. You can continue to perpetuate the feeling, including the anger and depression, or you can ask for the guidance to make it through another day and forge on. In doing so, you will be exercising your healing ability by choosing to push back and restart your determination.

Whenever you experience a setback, a naturally occurring bad day, *immediately refocus on your purpose*, your goal from the day before. This will make it easier to restart and keep going. Become aware of the thoughts that are bringing you down, and develop a scheme to dispatch them (for example, try substituting a thought about something in nature you love to see).

Nature Is an Eternal Healer

Better yet, get out into nature. Most mourners, as well as many who are not actively grieving, are "nature-deficient," staying indoors or away from others, day in and day out, due to work at their jobs or simply choosing to be inactive and away from others. Yet getting out in the sun, breathing clean air, seeing the colors and hearing the sounds of nature, and being on the move are all stress reducers and important for your health. Sun exposure also increases your vitamin D, which can help improve and regulate your moods.

Human Contact: A Must

Over thirty years ago, Dr. Richard Kalish, a well-known writer and thanatologist, offered this thought, which he said came from a clergyperson: "Truth minus love equals brutality. Love minus truth equals sentimentality. Truth plus love equals a healing relationship." This advice has many applications inside and outside of the grief process, as it does for those who care for the dying. This is a time when your truth plus love is needed.

If your faithful friend is not available, try a family member. Don't stay isolated for long periods of time. It will only make it worse. Go to where there is interaction and a peaceful atmosphere.

If there is a service at your local church or synagogue, consider attending. If that wouldn't work for you, get involved in a project that will take you outside the home where you won't be alone. Make the decision to connect with others as a way to manage this low point in your grief. And never forget: you can always have a new beginning. Grief is a series of new beginnings. Be assured, your bad days and nights will come to an end. You will feel better.

55. Speak to Your Loved One

It is not unusual for mourners to have a conversation with a deceased loved one. Time and time again, when I ask the bereaved if they speak to the deceased, the vast majority say they do. And there are benefits to such action, especially early in one's grief work. While at first glance you may think this is strange behavior, and friends may feel you are in need of professional help, millions of people do this year in and year out. It is an effective therapeutic outlet for the turmoil within, and many believe they are heard and receive comfort.

There are a considerable number of people who listen to the telephone answering machine with the loved one's voice, wear some of their clothing, or sleep in their bed—all healthy responses for those individuals. Others pray and talk to their deceased loved ones on a regular basis, sometimes every day, early in their grief. And no, it is not at all unusual, since the practice has a long history. In fact, some Christian denominations teach the doctrine of the Communion of Saints. This involves the belief that deceased loved ones, who are in heaven, are able to hear you and intercede with God for those on earth.

As for your friends and what they might think, I would suggest that is the last thing to worry about. If they consider it odd or unhealthy to be speaking to a deceased loved one, that is their problem, not yours. Let them crane their necks in surprise. Of course, you don't have to tell them anything and it is best to tell only those whom you believe will not judge you negatively.

I highly recommend to all people in my support groups to talk to the loved one whenever they feel comfortable doing so. Why? Because it has obvious benefits and it feeds the spiritual self. If you talk to your loved one, some remarkable things can occur, such as:

- It will provide an outlet and release as you deal with many changes in the days ahead. This opportunity will be perpetually present. For many people who talk to their deceased loved one, the action itself is comforting. They are doing something that eases the burden of accepting that the loved one is not physically present.

- It gives motivation to work toward adjusting to a new world. Having a real or imaginary conversation with a loved one, when dealing with massive change, may provide the extra push to deal with a difficult problem. If you believe your loved one can hear you (and millions do), then ask for help in tackling the problem—see what pops into your mind after asking a question. If you don't believe you are being heard, that you are simply using your imagination, then after asking a question, play along and imagine what your loved one might say in response.

- It is a way to demonstrate love in separation. Talking out loud or silently to your loved one is another example of remembrance. My mother died over thirty years ago, and I still talk to her. The deceased is always a thought away in your heart, and it may well be an important way for you to remind yourself that love never dies. Though separated, you will always have a relationship. There is nothing untoward with honoring the dead every day in this way, if you are so inclined.

- It can be a wake-up ritual. Rituals, whether formal or informal, provide a major way of establishing priorities or new routines when coping with loss. They are also a way of honoring the deceased. Starting the day off, as many survivors do, with greetings or remembrance to the deceased before getting into the hustle and bustle of the day is a hope-filled way to begin your day. Think of what your loved one would say back to you right now.

- It is an effective emotional release. Emotions are inner messengers telling us to find resolution to conflict. Many widows and widowers speak to their deceased spouses to express feelings, a critical human response. This action is not only mentally and physically appropriate but it allows a freedom for telling it like it is not often found when interacting with others. "It makes me feel he's still around," said one mourner.

- It bolsters much needed confidence. "I feel better," said one woman after speaking to her deceased loved one. Others suggest a talk can diminish the feeling of being alone. Still others use a conversation to ask for a sign that the loved one is okay in another existence.

- It promotes inner peace to be able to tell a loved one when something happens. When living alone, many widows talk to the deceased loved one, especially in the evenings when in need of companionship. Do what you feel comfortable with, and that gives peace of mind, which is a major factor in evaluating the awareness and use of mystery in a world steeped in the idea that "seeing is believing."

Even though we live in a world designed to keep the spiritual and the soulful on the periphery, it does not mean that we cannot intelligently choose to speak to a deceased loved one. No one can explain how this interaction may work, and it's not necessary to have an explanation. Sometimes mourners are convinced they have received an idea from their loved one after a good talk.

We know that spiritual traditions around the world suggest praying to deceased loved ones. The best-selling author Thomas Moore insightfully recalls part of his mother's legacy: "My mother honored the dead and communicated with her ancestors constantly. She taught me this piece of practical mystical theology, and I will continue to follow her way." You, your loved one, and your higher power make a union in love that is bound to bring comfort.

Depending on your belief system, incorporate conversations with your loved one and your higher power as a way to cope with your loss and reinvest in life. As a widow who was engaged to be remarried told me recently, "It's been over eight years and I still converse with him [her first husband]. I tell him to go out there and help our son." This woman is as grounded as anyone you would want to meet, and has learned to incorporate nonphysical reality into her lifestyle. You can too, and live life more fully.

56. Release Your Anger as a Gift to Yourself

Anger is a common part of grief for many people. If you feel anger, you're in a normal process. Anger has a role in telling us that something is not right, someone left or was taken, or someone may have overstepped reasonable boundaries. You may even be angry at the deceased for leaving you, which for some is difficult to understand. However, don't get angry at yourself; you are not a superman or superwoman. There are some things you just can't change.

We can always look back and say, I should have done this or that. Yet perpetually holding on to anger trashes your inner life. As a saying often attributed to Mark Twain has it: "Anger is an acid that can do more harm to the vessel in which it stands than to anything on which it is poured." Releasing anger means you are eliminating the conflict that is taking a deadly toll on your mind and body; anger is extremely bad for electrical conduction in the heart, according to cardiologists.

This does not mean anger is a bad emotion, because it can become a source of motivation for good actions and better thinking. In fact, knowing when to channel anger by releasing it, and knowing when it is good for you to suppress it and suck it up, is a crucial skill to develop. If you don't feel you have any anger, remember that it can secretly show up in jealousy, criticism, fear (often expressed through anger), subtle sarcasm, withdrawal, intolerance, and self-incriminating feelings.

But eventually, letting go of anger meets the objective of peace of mind. You realize that embracing anger and resentment is only damaging *you*, not the object of your anger. Carolyn Myss, a medical intuitive, put it this way: "Holding on to anger is like taking rat poison and expecting the other person to die." You are allowing another person or experience to hold power and control over you. Your goal in dealing with anger is to find a way to express it or decide you can just let it go.

57. Refuse to Hold a Grudge: Always Forgive

This is not easy to do. Prolonged anger or hate changes nothing—except your heart. You cannot love and heal when you are angry. Every time you replay the anger scene in your thoughts, your body pays the same stressful price at the cellular level as when you first experienced your anger. So examine anger as a cover for other feelings you are not dealing with. Often, holding a grudge leads to depression, sleepless nights, and much anxiety and tension. It's a no-win situation. Nothing good will come of it, with one exception: it can motivate you to positive action.

Sometimes walking away from the source of your anger, realizing the person needs to be loved, is useful. Replacing thoughts of anger with thoughts of love will guarantee to lessen your burden. Remember: this is self-care at its best, practicing much needed self-love by taking back control of your life through forgiveness. Think of whom you have to forgive, release them from your inner prison, and it will change the quality of your spiritual life.

OTHER IMMEDIATE
RELEASES FOR ANGER

▸ Remove yourself from whatever is the recall button for your anger. Move away from the scene or the person who is the reminder and say you need a timeout. Rating your anger and then resisting it can work in some situations. Sometimes we can hold it in, and at other times, we have to find an outlet.

▸ Focus exclusively on slowing down your breathing rate. Counting numbers may also be a choice for immediate control. Tell yourself to slow down and control the potential outburst.

▸ If your anger involves a friend or coworker, think through the background or forces behind that person's negative behavior. People often respond based on their low self-esteem. That one act is not the whole person. Everyone has limiting beliefs (part of their programming) affecting what they say or do, often for the worse. Then write a letter saying what you feel, but don't mail it. Burn it as a way of saying, "I'm letting this go." Follow that with the most difficult part: feeling compassion for the person who hurt you.

▸ Look for physical outlets for the stored-up anger through exercise. Anything that will increase your heart rate through motion or stretching will be an outlet. If alone, even a good scream can give immediate release and time to work on reducing anger intensity.

▸ Consider channeling your anger into a positive outlet, a protest, or an organization.

▸ Place yourself in the shoes of the person who is the focus of your anger. This is especially important because often you can then find a reason to forgive. For example, realizing human weakness and reasoning as to why certain things were said or done can be useful. What issues is the person dealing with? Accept the fact that we are all imperfect. Ask yourself what you would tell a friend who came to you for advice in dealing with the anger you are harboring. Then take your own advice.

Choose the forgiveness path by awakening to the fact that to forgive does not mean you condone, accept, or justify the wrong. Through forgiveness you recognize that the behavior of another, the cause of your anger, is that person's problem and responsibility, not yours. Sure, that person started it. You can finish it in the right way, get rid of the negative energy engulfing you, and protect yourself. What you will gain will be unheralded freedom to live whole and focus on the good parts of your life. This is especially true if you are constantly dwelling on the topic of whose fault it was.

Tell a trusted confidant exactly why you are angry. Get the whole story out one final time, so you can take the next important step of letting it go. Give it a final release by punching a pillow, kicking a soccer ball, or finding a place where you can be alone and talk it out. Say "I am letting this go" as you make a motion as if throwing something away. Or use the approach of thinking of the person as having made a serious mistake, as we all do at various times.

If you are depressed or feeling down, forgiving will be a crucial component of yanking you out of this downward spiral, especially if you are angry at yourself.

If your anger, frustration, and disappointment are with God, you can forgive Him too. As a wise mentor of mine once said when talking about anger at God, "He can take it. He understands better than anyone else when you are thinking thoughts of 'Where were you when I needed you?'"

Not only will forgiving help your relationship, ability to love, and your prayer life, but you will be better able to listen to your intuitive voice. You will never work through your loss if you keep alive the bitterness in your heart. By refusing to forgive, you guarantee you will hold on to your loss too tightly and likely use grief as a badge of honor. Reflect on your own miscues that have angered others, and realize we are all mortals who make lots of errors.

It is easier to forgive with your intellect, but it will take much longer to forgive from your heart. Commit to making the start. Practice what you will say and decide where would be the best place to say it. And know you have the most to gain. When you forgive, it does not mean you must forget or pretend you are not hurt, although they are noble goals. Gradually you can distance yourself from the hurt as the love in your heart grows.

58. Have "Remember When" Sessions

Memories are powerful grieving tools as well as long-term sources of comfort for the rest of your life. An important way to recognize and honor your loved one is to have "remember when" sessions. These are nothing more than celebratory stories from the past involving your loved one. The important point is that "remembering when" becomes an easy way to keep wise, happy, or funny memories of the loved one alive, as well as learn a few new ones from others.

For example, after the death of my father-in-law, on the anniversary of his death, we would go out for dinner. My mother-in-law would take us to a local restaurant. When it came time to pay the bill and I would fumble for my wallet, she would say, "This is on Al [her husband]." We would all chuckle. But that opened up conversation about him and where he liked to eat, etc. We were all willing to talk about him; it was healthy and acceptable.

Try Some Mental Time Travel

Throughout the year there are a number of times when a birthday, holiday, or special event occurs which would have normally involved the deceased. These get-togethers are all great opportunities to casually start talking about the deceased with family members or friends and tell stories about events that can be funny or descriptive of a loving memory. You can even solicit stories from all who are present and ask each to tell something they remember about the loved one. Simply say, "What is one of your favorite stories about_____?" Don't miss these occasions to remember and highlight some of the lessons learned from your deceased loved one.

Some family members or friends may be fearful of upsetting you by talking about the deceased. You will have to start this new tradition, as my mother-in-law did, and make it clear that it's okay to talk about the loved one. This is especially important on significant anniversaries and holidays.

59. Accept the Strange Feeling of Relief

It is not unusual, if you have spent months or years caring for your loved one, to feel a sense of relief when those duties have come to an end. This feeling is a normal response after being under the constant pressure of caregiving. In fact, you may be at a loss about what to do with all of the time you have on your hands. Now is when you can begin exploring old interests and develop some new ones that will bring a sense of achievement and challenge back into your life.

Again, it will be useful to tell someone about this feeling of relief, especially if you have any pangs of guilt.

60. Find a Way to Say Goodbye, If Needed

Because of the individuality of grieving, some mourners have to say a series of good-byes over a long period of time. Others may not need a continuing bond, for whatever reason. Sometimes the need to say goodbye or to give permission to the loved one to let go was not met. You may have been away when the death occurred, or death may have been due to a sudden unexpected event. Many survivors are guilt-ridden over this, when in fact there is clearly no outward cause for such guilt, because the event was beyond their control. Realize you are not responsible. Yet unexpected death often wipes out our ability to see that we did not create the circumstances that cause the emotion being experienced.

Consider the following: sometimes dying people choose to die when those close to them are not present in order to spare survivors additional pain. Many medical people believe that some dying people are able to choose when they leave their bodies. Also, it is not uncommon for a person to die in a hospital or hospice setting when a family member is rushing to get there. All of the pain of these events is maximized by the thought of not being with the person at the end.

So what can be done to reduce emotional pain and provide support in the face of deep sadness? Plenty. One or more of the following can prove helpful.

Say Goodbye in a Private Setting

I often tell those who are mourning the death of a loved one that there is nothing wrong with talking to the person who has died. Say how you feel about not being there at the time of their death. It is a successful coping response used by millions of people and a meaningful way to say a temporary farewell.

Find a quiet room in your home, place a picture or other symbol of the loved one across from you, and say whatever you need to say. Explain why you were not there, why you are sorry, and that your love will always be with the person. If you believe in an afterlife, ask the person to send you a sign that they have heard you and are okay. Then stay alert for a response in the days or weeks ahead.

Try Writing Your Good-byes

Writing thoughts and descriptions of feelings can provide a profound emotional and physical release. Write as though you are speaking directly to the person and be specific. Put an "I love you" in it, and write that you will never forget your loved one. When you are burdened by your thoughts of not having said goodbye, reread what you have written. You may also want to add something else that you believe is important to your writing at this time.

Write or paste messages to the loved one on a biodegradable helium-filled balloon for release. This can be a wonderful opportunity for a ritual of goodbye as you watch the balloon ascend into the sky. It will give you a planned occasion to think of your loved one, if you are alone, or discuss memories of the loved one, if it is a group or family ritual. Be sure you purchase a biodegradable balloon, as others are a hazard to wildlife and the environment.

Focus On a Memory

Go to a church, synagogue, or mosque, or out into a beautiful natural setting. Go where you feel the sacred. Meditate on the belief that the loved one understands the circumstances surrounding your inability to say goodbye and would not hold a grudge. Then divert your awareness to a pleasant memory of the deceased, or him or her saying "I forgive you." This technique is a powerful coping response to develop, and can be used for dealing with many other unwanted thoughts. Remember, confronting unwanted thoughts with a strategy, though painful, will reduce the frequency of their appearance. Meditate, assume loving forgiveness, and let them go.

These approaches for dealing with not being able to say goodbye have a common goal: the acceptance of one of the sad events often associated with the death of a loved one. In the final analysis, each person has the ability to say a belated goodbye, let go of anxiety, recognize that separations without good-byes happen often, and start on the long road of reinvesting in life.

61. Recognize the Need to Heal Your Disenfranchised Grief

Disenfranchised grief is what mourners experience when their losses are not socially recognized or sanctioned and given the status of culturally recognized losses; therefore they are not publicly mourned. In some cultural circles this means losses of pets, ex-spouses, aborted babies, the AIDS-deceased, or lovers who are not recognized by many as having close relationships, necessitating a strong grief response. It could also include coworkers or any unsanctioned relationship.

What nonsense. The degree of emotional investment in a person, pet, or other object of loss is only known to the primary mourners. Often, disenfranchised grief means that formal rituals, so important when grieving, are limited or nonexistent. Yet great support is needed. This is especially so if other disenfranchised losses have preceded the present one.

I once had a young woman come up to me on campus who was mourning the deaths of her goldfish. Some would laugh at this, but it was not a laughing matter. There was no one she could turn to out of fear that they would think she needed serious counseling. She needed someone who would validate her loss, which I did. Likewise, the death of a companion animal can evoke grief that is as difficult to work through as the death of a relative or friend; sometimes even more so, primarily because our relationship with a companion animal is normally much less ambivalent than a human relationship.

Disenfranchised grief may also occur to professional caregivers after the death of a patient. Few realize the quality of relationships that can develop between the two. Doctors as well as nurses often need someone who will recognize and legitimize their grief. There are many other instances in which grief is not recognized by those who could assist the bereaved. For example, some mourners are ashamed by the cause of death of a loved one (such as AIDS) and do not seek assistance, and some are excluded from funeral services. The developmentally disabled are another group often overlooked. The world is full of hidden sorrow, and if you are hiding yours, you are adding a major complication to the process of adapting.

WHAT CAN YOU DO IF YOUR GRIEF IS DISENFRANCHISED?

Two chief characteristics of disenfranchised grief are that much goes unrecognized in terms of depth of feelings, and therefore, adequate support is lacking. Obviously, you must find people, either lay or professional, who understand the nature of your relationship to the deceased and realize the legitimacy of the grief you are experiencing. These individuals and that understanding are out there in your community. You may have to consult the Internet in some situations for help. Whatever you do, don't add to your suffering by trying to go it alone. Make your sorrow known.

With the assistance of those who understand your legitimate pain and suffering, determine ways to express your emotions and create rituals appropriate to the circumstances. For example, if the death was of a pet, you may want to walk the same route and talk about your lost companion with a trusted friend. Rituals, both formal and informal, can have a number of meanings, some of which are not apparent until we go through the ritual and feel the results of participation. It is essential that you find a way to acknowledge the death.

Consider ways to memorialize the loved one. As with any death, disenfranchised survivors need ways to keep the memory of the deceased alive. Memorials reflect our creative individuality and may include objects, pictures, visits to certain vacation sites, or carrying on a tradition started by the deceased. Let your heart be your guide in this important endeavor.

Deal with guilt. If you have feelings of guilt associated with the death (which often occurs) due to the nature of your relationship with the deceased or the type of death, look for professional assistance. Disenfranchised grief is complicated grief, usually demanding much long-term care and processing. Be willing to go to a grief counselor who can help with self-forgiveness, realistic expectations, and determining whether the guilt is neurotic or truly cause-and-effect in nature.

62. Accept Your Grief Triggers

Have you been having a good day many weeks or months after the death of your loved one and, when watching television, seen a particular scene or heard a statement, and suddenly you felt the return of sadness and anxiety? Or has a newspaper story of the death of a stranger set off sorrowful memories associated with the death of your loved one?

These and many other seemingly unrelated experiences commonly cause much grieving that can go on for several days. Kim Wencl, whose daughter died in a tragic house fire while at college, had the following experience:

> The bridge collapse in Minneapolis was a trigger for me. It really had nothing to do with my loss (although when my daughter was attending the University of Minnesota we traveled it quite frequently, and many of her college friends still live within close proximity to it). But as soon as I heard about it and started to watch the news coverage, I felt almost physically ill and panicky, had difficulty breathing, and experienced immediate and immense feelings of extreme sadness. Despite all of these feelings, I couldn't get myself to quit watching the coverage—even though after a couple of hours, I realized it was triggering my own grief feelings, which hadn't bubbled up in almost a year. If you don't know what a trigger is (and I don't think most grieving people

do), it is even more unnerving because it comes out of the blue, very quickly, and you don't understand why it's happening.

Make a list of your grief triggers as they occur, so you can practice prevention when possible. You won't be able to prevent all of them, but you can substantially reduce their number through avoiding the sources. Here's what you need to know when something you see, hear, smell, or experience brings back the full pain of your loss:

1. The experience is normal and common. There is nothing wrong with you. You did not cause the event. It is part of the way we store memories and the automatic response of patterned thinking. Recall what you read in chapter 2, that how we respond to an event depends on the thought and the feeling it arouses. We can follow through with an automatic response—or change it. Sometimes it is the result of unresolved traumatic imprints—highly emotional events that become embedded in our psyches and our bodies and may need professional assistance to manage. Both happy and not-so-happy memories have their triggers. The role of the mind in healing is extremely powerful and at other times extremely limiting. Expect grief triggers; that's the way memory works.

2. To help defuse the impact of the sudden onset of grief (a grief attack), keep telling yourself that what you are experiencing

is normal, normal, normal. Say it to yourself: affirming this belief will expand your ability to continue healing. *You can create a modified pattern of thinking, feeling, and responding.* Deal with it by expressing your emotions and finding support from persons who understand the phenomenon and your need for their active listening skills. Regrettably, you may have to explain your behavior to some of them at this difficult time. Nevertheless, full disclosure of what is happening within can be useful in self-management. Don't hide your feelings. You are not weak in sharing your plight.

3. Remember that these grief episodes, like all grief responses, have a physical component. You can get a headache, digestive disturbances, feel ill, or not be able to sleep. Thoughts are always transferred to our cells with corresponding physical manifestations. Of course, from the modern perspective of neurochemistry, this also means that joyful and peaceful thoughts can have highly positive effects on your physiology, especially the immune system. In fact, *all positive emotions are associated with healthy immune system function, just as negative emotions stress it.*

4. Allow the experience to unfold and the pain in your heart to move through and out of you. Here is how Kim put it: "As to what helped in dealing with that grief trigger experience, I guess the biggest thing was just knowing that what I was experiencing was a grief trigger. Once I had that realization, I knew that, if I acknowledged everything I was feeling and just felt it—as opposed to ignoring it or pretending

it wasn't happening—the symptoms would subside, which they did over the course of a day or two." The key words in this observation are "acknowledge everything."

Finally, I can't emphasize enough how individualistic grief triggers can be. The intensity, extent, and frequency of these events vary immensely among individuals. Depending on the circumstances surrounding the death of your loved one, the emotional investment in the person, and the internal connections made from your precipitating experience—a grief trigger for you may be a complete surprise and thus alarming.

In any event, accepting the experience and not resisting is the best way to disarm and limit the unnecessary suffering that accompanies this loss-related grief response. The transition will require you to shift your thought processes away from focusing on "why me?" to "what can I learn from this experience?"

Accepting grief triggers as normal—especially when they come months or years after the death of your loved one—is a manageable and ongoing part of the healing process. We are always healing because we are always dealing with change. And we bring with us our previous loss experiences to each new challenge. You can meet that challenge.

63. Work Toward Accepting the Uncertainty of Ambiguous Loss

Ambiguous losses involve a lack of certainty that a loved one has died. Someone is missing in an accident at sea. A soldier's body is never found after action in a war zone. A child disappears without a trace while hiking. An adult is caught in a mountain avalanche. Ambiguous losses may be psychological as well as physical. They may last for a week or the rest of one's life.

As a former consultant to an alcohol referral service, I saw many families who had absentee alcoholic fathers or mothers, even though both parents were living under the same roof. A spouse or several children were always uncertain about when or if the person would be home, and in what condition. Addictions to various drugs bring ongoing sadness and long-term grief for family members. Psychological loss of a person can be every bit as damaging as physical absence. Alzheimer's disease and comas induced by accidents are other examples of physical presence but uncertain psychological presence. All are grief-producing.

These events can have several possible results. They are not only shrouded in uncertainty and show no signs of ending but in some instances are lifelong stressors for survivors. They are much more prevalent than the general public realizes, and cause much more confusion for would-be caregivers who try to provide support.

What can you do if you are mourning an ambiguous loss?

Your troubling emotions and physical stress, ever present, are to be expected, since the usual predictable and assuring factors that bring some sense of security or knowledge are absent. Frequent antistress measures to deal with fear and insecurity are critically important in managing any type of ambiguous loss. Diversions are essential, as you can easily become immobilized and stuck in your grief.

Recognize that social dislocation and perceptual differences in viewing ambiguous loss are common threads. For example, children of a family who have been deserted by a parent may feel different toward that parent or have an opposite view of the remaining parent who is still in the home. In other families with a missing member, one person may feel the person who has not been found has died, while another holds out hope that the person will be found alive.

More than ever, if you are dealing with ambiguous loss of any type, find a grief professional for guidance. There are counselors who have much expertise in this area, and can help you sort out feelings and look at the pros and cons of taking specific actions depending on the nature of the loss. Discover the ways others have dealt with uncertain losses, take and use what rings true for you, and let the rest go for the present time.

Learning to live with uncertainty and insecurity is your goal, as impossible as it may seem. This is a form of acceptance of your great loss. Know that others have done it.

Look for reassurance from all of the resources in your community, beginning with those who have experience with these types of losses. New ways of looking at the world are needed, and you will need highly individual coping strategies to deal with your brand of uncertainty. Believe you will find a way that works for you, as many before you have. Equally important, social interaction and relying on your spiritual traditions are necessary. Over time, changing your perception of any event can prove to be a highly successful coping strategy.

Most important of all, be open in communication with family members. Having had two divorces within my own family, I know this is not always easy to do. Yet airing differences with patience and respect, coupled with complete disclosure, can be most helpful, especially for the children. Recognize that as the months and years go by symbolic remembrances are important, bouts of loneliness will be common, reevaluation of relationships can be useful, and the resiliency of the people involved will be evident.

64. Facilitate Needed Sleep

Sleep is hard to come by, particularly in the early days and weeks of mourning. However, there is much you can do to get your needed rest. Without it, you will quickly lose energy and be easily susceptible to a variety of sleep deprivation ailments, not to mention a weakened immune system. Here are some recommendations that you can utilize:

- As difficult as it is, after the funeral, try to go to bed at the same time each evening to reestablish your shut-eye pattern. Getting back to your old schedule is good here, unless it brings back a particularly sad memory involving the deceased loved one. If so, A slight change in time might be appropriate. If unable to sleep, get up, do something, and then try going back to bed again.

- Your daily walk will facilitate going to bed at your normal time. Plan a specific time each day to stimulate your physiology with a brisk twenty-minute walk. Make it longer if you have the energy. However, make sure your exercise plan is a good three hours before bedtime, as your body needs time to unwind.

- It can help to meditate or do some reading an hour before bedtime to help calm down. Shut off all radios and televisions. Once in bed, make every attempt to hand all worry over to your higher power.

- Stop caffeine consumption after 3:00 p.m. and avoid snacks, especially sugary foods and grains before bedtime.

- Be sure your room is completely dark and all light from the outside is kept out with drapes or blinds. Light can block needed melatonin production. When you have to get up to go to the bathroom, use a penlight or book-light to find your way to the bathroom door. Or put a nightlight in the bathroom and leave the door partially open.

- Do not watch TV or use your computer while lying in bed. Make your bedroom for sleep only. Remove your computer from the bedroom, if that's where you have it.

- Once in bed, take some deep abdominal breaths, inhaling slowly through the nose, holding for a three-count, and exhaling for a four-count slowly through the mouth in order to get your body to slow down. (See **#90, Use a Breathing Technique to Intervene in Your Stress Response**.) Next use the gratitude memories review discussed in **#88, Build a Data Bank of Gratitude Memories**, to help you fall off to sleep.

- It will help to have a sleep mask available if you are awake at the crack of dawn, especially if you do not have blackout curtains or drapes in your bedroom. Use it and try to go back off to sleep. Again, try thinking of gratitude memories.

- It is worth trying herbal sleep remedies such as valerian, hops, lemon balm, and passionflower. There are also preparations of melatonin (produced by the pineal gland to regulate sleep patterns) and 5-HTP (a byproduct of tryptophan, an amino acid that helps produce the feel-good molecule serotonin for relaxation) that have proven helpful. Tart cherries or cherry juice (no sugar) are also rich in melatonin and may help your insomnia.

- As unusual as it may seem, try wearing socks to bed. Increased blood flow from warmth in the extremities induces sleep for many. I often do this during the winter months.

- If you are always worrying or thinking about what you must do tomorrow, place a pen and paper on your nightstand. Thoroughly write up each item, then let them go, so you can go off to sleep knowing you can tackle them tomorrow.

65. Talk about Secrets Discovered after Death

Everyone lives with secrets. Some of them stay inside of us forever, and no one, not even our closest confidant, ever finds out about them. It is not uncommon to find out something about a loved one who died and be shocked or dismayed by the finding. It could be something good (an award, a thank-you or love note, a hobby, etc.) that was not shared, or something not so good (a love note to someone else, gambling debt, an addiction, or something about their past) that was covered up. Some secrets bring an added feeling of pride in your loved one, others an additional loss to be grieved and much more shock and sadness.

There are instances, where the secret has to do with an indiscretion, an affair, a secret trip, or something from the past that had never been revealed. What can be done, if this has happened to you? First, assuming you have all the facts, find a confidant and talk about how you are feeling because of your discovery. This is an essential action to take. Most secrets generate additional questions and considerations that need to be addressed and mulled over with the trusted friend. Secrets found out are often strong secondary losses. They need to be grieved when interpreted as a betrayal of trust.

Next, remember we are all imperfect and make bad choices and mistakes, for whatever reasons. Consider the background or upbringing that could prompt the behavior. Give the loved one the benefit of the doubt and remember that there were so many good things that came from knowing your loved one. He or she is so much more than the secret. We are never just our behavior. It is a fact of life that we often cannot find out everything about those we love. Once more, it is quite common that we never know everything about someone else, whether a spouse or sibling.

Make a list of all you received from knowing him or her. Your attention to this list will dwarf the secret. When it comes up periodically in your thinking, allow your emotions to flow when necessary. This is a normal human response, given the circumstances. At some point, you may need to forgive and let it remain part of the past. Not to forgive is to continue to punish yourself.

66. Begin a Twenty-Minute Daily Meditation Period

What can twenty minutes of daily meditation do for you? First and foremost, it will alter the functioning of your brain so you can release some of the stress you are experiencing and increase awareness and attention span. Our level of awareness narrows when we are mourning.

Erase the old image that meditation is a far-out practice for dropouts. Practicing meditation can have numerous benefits, and you do not have to believe in a specific religion to meditate. The truth of the matter is physicians throughout the country are beginning to recognize the value of meditation for treating depression. In addition, it has been shown to:

• Reduce high blood pressure, dilate blood vessels, and protect the heart
• Improve sleep and immune function
• Increase focus and concentration

- Bring calmness into your life and the ability to relax
- Increase self-acceptance and longevity
- Lower anxiety and decrease panic attacks
- Give you a tool to increase your intuitive ability
- Provide spiritual insights
- Strengthen relationships with others

You don't have to spend loads of time meditating. Twenty minutes a day will do. If you feel that is too long, start with ten minutes and increase it, until a few days later you are at twenty. It will not only alter brain function for the better; it can relieve headaches and gastrointestinal distress.

Four Types of Meditation

Here are four types of meditation you can try. The process for one of the most common, *breathing meditation*, is simple:

- Create a sacred place in one corner of a room in your home. Add a comfortable chair.
- Surround yourself with things that bring loving memories, such as pictures and mementos. These are life-giving.
- Close your eyes and start the meditation process by inhaling through your nose.
- Focus on a word ("heal," "love," "peace," "release," etc.), and slowly repeat it each time you exhale. When thoughts intrude that you don't like, gently refocus on your breathing and release them.

A second form is *walking meditation*, where your intent is to focus on the feelings in your body as you walk. Focus also on what you see and smell in nature and feel in your body, not on your destination or how long it will take to get there.

Binaural audio programs can also bring excellent results, as good as any meditative practice. You can buy a CD or MP3 player with headphones, find a quiet spot where you won't be disturbed, and allow different tone frequencies to lower your brainwaves.

Pray, meditate, and reaffirm your determination to transcend your loss as part of your meditation process. Use this Mother Teresa prayer: "The fruit of silence is prayer. The fruit of prayer is faith. The fruit of faith is love. The fruit of love is service. The fruit of service is peace." Look at meditation as one of your peaceful healers.

Finally you can use *guided meditations* for a specific purpose of your choice, as there is a variety to choose from. These recordings can be most effective, especially if you can connect with the voice tone.

When your mind wanders, as it normally will, gently bring it back and focus on your intention. You can also use a favorite scene or a spiritual being as the source of your focus in breathing meditation. Or focus on someone you love.

Yes, there are times when we think too much and our minds are racing. Let go for a while, through healing meditation. It will affect the way you relate to your loss and present new insights. The goal is to get away from it all and just be and let the mystery flow through you.

67. Be Mindful of What You Focus Your Attention On

Awakening to the incontrovertible fact that *constant attention* to your loss increases pain will go a long way toward reducing the impact of hurtful thoughts that accompany all loss experiences. This holds true for fear as well as negative inner chatter. Why? *Because a narrow focus takes away the big picture.* Thus we bring into our lives that which we continually focus on. Attention is just as powerful for visualizing, meeting, and successfully negotiating a particular problem as it is for increasing suffering. Kathy Valente, a bereaved mother who talked and wrote to me about her son, wisely put it this way:

> You can only have one thought at a time, so when you get the negative thoughts, which you do get constantly in the first year, you have to immediately do what I call "change the channel." Sometimes I just want to feel the sadness, so I choose not to change the channel, but I know that I do have control. Dwelling is dangerous. If you dwell on the past, you will have no future, but if you dwell on the future, you will have the past. It has worked for me. I loved my twenty-two-year-old son more than life, and my greatest and last gift to him is my happiness. I'm happy. I tell others that they MUST have faith and know that we will be with [our loved ones] again.

Consciously Shift Your Focus

You can be proactive and strengthen your ability to eliminate unnecessary suffering. The question to remember is "Where am I putting my attention?" Full attention on a positive memory or a gratitude memory will reduce pain time. These positive events will expand in importance and assist your transition.

For example, think of a time when you felt loved. Relive the scene in detail, whether it was when you were a child or an adult. Dwell on the place, event, and person or persons involved. Keep focusing on it and experience how it relaxes your body. Write it up in your journal or diary to reread later. Become aware of where you direct your attention and start spending more time and focused thought on what is working for you.

On the other hand, if you are living on a diet of ANTs (automatic negative thoughts), your attitude, emotions, and ultimately your behavior becomes infected with this poison. Fear, for example, increases as you continue your focus on it instead of sharing it, accepting it as a lack-of-control problem, facing it, and telling yourself you will deal with it in time. *Recognize that unwanted thoughts are a normal part of grief work.* Letting them leave as they have entered is an effective strategy. Refuse to give them the attention they thrive on.

It has long been known that *the more you focus on pain, the more pain you attract.* Every time the realization hits you that he or she is gone, after a short period of time, have something you can refocus your thoughts on to take away some of the increasing power you are giving to sadness and pain. Squash pessimism by switching gears. Using a word or phrase as a signal to refocus is an effective tool in this self-conditioning.

Also, make every effort to recall a positive memory to reroute thoughts and feelings. These are moments of transformation through focused thought. Accept the fact that we all have highs and lows, and when these depressing times show up, imagine them as a normal part of having to deal with major transitions. Don't overreact to the fact that you are having these experiences; it's part of the territory. Allow them to only be temporary, as long as you want them, and then go to work on dispatching them when they become overburdening.

You always have the choice of what thoughts, attitudes, and emotions you will allow to stay in your mind. You are in charge. Never give up your personal power to shape the course of the journey through grief by worrying about the future or what has happened. Your power lies in the present moment, not in the past or the future, which you cannot control.

Reprogram Your Powerful Unconscious Mind

Create in your mind's eye the end result desired until you feel you are living it. This is where forward-thinking action is permissible. Be sure to add the emotions that would normally be involved. Emotion will help plant it in your unconscious mind and help you act as you eventually wish to be. When other images crowd in that are in opposition to the desired outcome, dispatch them immediately, especially pessimistic thoughts. Pull the switch and reprogram.

You must understand that your unconscious mind *automatically accepts without question or judgment* the thoughts and emotions you feed it—that inner faculty will support more of the same—reinforcing and adding to all of the negativity on a conscious level.

Again, this is an ongoing and automatic process that you must actively short-circuit. Your unconscious *never* takes a break, does not distinguish between reality and wishful thinking, and will continue to play your childhood program. As children, we observe and automatically file everything in the unconscious—and it affects adult behavior. However, you can break the automatic cycle by updating and reprogramming the way the unconscious responds. Here's how: create specific mental images of one thing you want to accomplish this day or week as you grieve. Keep repeating the specific images and appropriate affirmations.

Your unconscious mind works when you don't know it, and that is all of the time; it constantly takes in and processes large amounts of information. Its functions affect your physiology all day every day, as well as your achievements. It is the difference between success or failure at various points in your grief work. Whatever your conscious mind thinks and focuses on, the unconscious takes to heart and goes for. Pour in habitually devastating thoughts and beliefs from the past, and you continually plant the seeds of nonstop sorrow. Plant "I am getting through this" thoughts—with strong emotion attached—and you'll get adaptive opportunities galore.

Ways to consciously break the cycle and rewrite your program are through progressive muscle relaxation, positive inner dialogue, changing habits, visualization, habitual focus on all the good things in your environment (a big one), exercise, automatic thought stopping, taking action, and meditation. (See **#15, Silence Your Rude and Frightening Inner Voice**, and **#90, Use a Breathing Technique to Intervene in Your Stress Response**.)

68. Don't Rule Out Happiness

I have already written about not grieving 24/7, and later you will read about having a balancing list of activities (see **#96, Determine What Recharges You**) you can turn to in taking a break from the stress of grief. Happiness is an altogether different condition; it is a level of consciousness that is still attainable even though the awareness of your loss is forever etched in your memory. It will always be there, and that's okay. Thus it is not unusual to think, "I will never be happy again."

To heal and find some semblance of happiness, or not to heal, is one of the critical choices of the grief process that comes many months, even years, after the death of our loved ones. The idea of happiness will invade your thoughts early on, and you may quickly dismiss it as ridiculous. You continually focus on what you miss.

Why then do I consider not ruling out happiness as a survival skill? Because it is wise to consider what happiness means and whether your deceased loved one would want you to continue to grieve and withdraw for the rest of your life. I have heard many mourners say they were motivated to enjoy life again because that is exactly what the deceased would want for them. They take seriously and choose to follow the example of their loved one. Some of our loved ones, dying, give us the gift of telling us they want us to be happy. Whether or not they say it, that is what all of our loved ones would want. So take the gift of knowing your loved one would want you to live your life and *do so as a tribute to him or her*.

Happiness Is Not a Destination

The experts on happiness say it is a *process* built on close relationships, accomplishing goals, caring, achievement, and the spirit of service. In short, it is primarily about what you do and think; it is in the act of doing that happiness suddenly appears. Happiness is another freebie that comes from meaningful connections and feeling needed—something we all seek. It also changes your energy for the better.

Do not underestimate the power of whom and what you connect with, including your deceased loved one, to help you live again. Be open to receiving and giving the benefits. You can't adapt to your greater good if you unconditionally say no to an incomplete idea of happiness and embrace the myth that it is a destination. Not gonna happen. Life will always keep offering opportunities to positively influence your world and those in it. So remember, happiness is all about doing, doing, doing.

Behind all of what I have said, happiness revolves around love and understanding needs, yours and the needs of those you interact with. "Life's greatest happiness," observed Victor Hugo, "is to be convinced we are loved." That goes for you as well as those who are in your social circle. Can you guess what you are bound to draw into your life if you decide to love on an unconditional basis?

69. Delegate: Don't Overdo It

This is another way of saying reach out and ask for help, at a time when asking for help is the normal human response. If you are the type of person who believes you have to do things in order to ensure they are done correctly, now is the time to back off on that belief and give yourself needed relief. Be willing to ask children, siblings, or friends to take care of specific tasks. You have too much on your mind not to allow yourself the temporary luxury of handing some responsibilities off to family members and friends as needed.

When it comes to tasks where professional expertise can provide assistance, take the opportunity to lighten your burden. Ask the advice of a counselor, nurse, physician, attorney, or financial consultant, and when possible allow them to do the job unimpeded. Many mourners who constantly push themselves and/or fret over a variety of loss-related tasks commonly end up with sleepless nights and eventually an illness that could have been prevented.

70. Use the Expressive Arts

I once interviewed a woman whose brother had died unexpectedly. She was, to say the least, an exceptional artist. Her paintings fetched high prices and hung in many banks and other venues. I was interviewing her because she had an extraordinary experience involving her brother. Since he had died, as a way of remembering and honoring him, in most of her subsequent paintings she had cleverly included the face of her brother in the background. It was not easy to see unless you were specifically looking for it—but she could see it clearly and knew it was there. The point is: for her it was a part of her grief work and, most importantly, an expression of loving in separation.

You do not have to be exceptionally talented to use the creative arts to express your grief or to honor your deceased loved one. If you draw, paint, sculpt, dance, or make crafts, you can use these mediums as a mode of expression, especially if you have trouble crying. Practicing an art interrupts negative thought patterns. Even if you feel you are not talented, you can learn to use movement therapy, drama, music, photo therapy, the visual arts, and writing poetry in imaginative ways to tell stories or create symbols (a single word could be a symbol) that have special meaning to you. In these forms, by using the language of your inner self, you can say what needs to be said to your loved one and to the world. Confer with an expressive arts therapist who can give you ideas on how to proceed. Go to the Internet to find therapists in your area.

71. Work to Become Interdependent

This does not mean you are solely dependent on anyone. It means you decide to join with, cooperate with, and build more together with others than you would by yourself. The satisfaction you obtain will soothe some of the residual hurt that often resurfaces from your great loss. Through collaboration, you can thrive despite loss; it works every time. Look at your skills and strengths, your work habits, or hobbies—your treasures. Think of ways you can integrate talents and insights in reaching common goals. Take action by joining community or self-help groups where you make a contribution along with others who have similar interests, values, and pursuits. Realize we are here to help each other and reap the benefits of purpose-driven cooperation.

I want to recommend that you consider forming a group of those who have grieved loved ones. Meet weekly or biweekly. Discuss difficulties of the past week, something good that happened during the week, what you missed most during the week, and what has been most helpful in coping with the absence of your loved one.

72. Be Aware of What You Watch and Listen To

The airways are filled with negative stories and information that can add immeasurably to your pain and suffering. You may turn on the news first thing in the morning and start your day with more sadness. Reduce this unnecessary overload by carefully selecting the programs you listen to and temporarily avoid those who seem to traffic in the saddest stories they can find. Media poison is often described as "If it bleeds, it leads." Constant exposure to uninspiring programming will have an impact on you, even if you are not giving it your full attention. Create the experience that you want by selectively choosing uplifting programs on channels you have not frequented before.

Be especially vigilant at night before going to sleep about what you watch on television and listen to on the radio. Sad thoughts generated from outside sources only add to the weight of grief, and they need to be recognized and their source eliminated. Although your unconscious mind takes in everything you are exposed to during the day, what reaches it in the evening can have a deleterious effect on sleep and dreams.

Limit the additional negativity by switching programs to an easy-listening music channel and away from the daily menu of mayhem flooding TV screens. Step out of the stressful atmosphere created by the media and take charge of what you allow to get into your thought processes. Don't let anyone else do your thinking for you, in a direct or indirect manner. When you find something delightful or soothing, allow the thoughts created to flow freely by increasing your focus on them.

BE GENTLE WITH YOURSELF

The key word here is "gentle." Ask yourself, when was the last time you were the priority, where you deliberately chose to do something for your own good? If you have been neglecting self-care, it will clearly affect the way you are coping with your loss. It is an important part of adjusting to any major loss that you be especially gentle with yourself when mistakes occur or something in the media upsets you.

Get away from the source of distress and create a more positive environment. Constant monitoring of what you allow from the outside to influence your inner life is a must. You have control over where to place your attention. And where your attention goes, there goes your energy. Let your attention be on pleasant thoughts for a part of every day, and it will have an immediate impact on your thought life and how you feel physically.

73. Take Your Time in Disposing of Your Loved One's Clothes and Possessions

There is usually a tendency to rush to dispose of clothing and possessions of the loved one. Often this is prompted by well-meaning friends and family members. There is no hard and fast rule to apply here. Go at your own pace, when you are ready. If seeing certain objects or pieces of clothing cause you deep sadness, put them aside and deal with them at a later date. If the thought of doing something with possessions is disturbing, again leave the task for another time. It all depends on what you want.

At an appropriate time, you may want to give some things to family members as a memory reminder or to your loved one's favorite charity. Or keep a particular object for display in your home to honor the deceased. There may be a piece of clothing that you always liked, and there is no reason why you can't keep it for its memory value. It may even carry the distinct smell that you associate with your loved one. All of this is healthy and part of your healing and acknowledgment of your great loss.

74. Bring Living Things into Your Life

As I said earlier, isolation leads to many detrimental effects on mind and body. Yet there are many hours when you have to be alone in your home or apartment. Do what you can to bring life there. It may mean getting a cat or a dog, or at least telling your friends you will be willing to be a sitter for their pet while they are away on a trip. Also, buy some plants or flowers that you can care for, grow, and then give away so you can grow some more. Consider a goldfish or a parakeet. Think of other living things that you might want to have at home and that you can care for. Put a vase of your favorite flowers on a table next to your bed so that they are one of the first things you see on awakening.

Taking care of plants, flowers, a garden, or a pet would be a good routine to establish. More important, though, is the satisfaction and comfort this action will bring. Those living alone have often found the companionship of a pet, usually a dog or a cat, to be especially helpful in the evenings and weekends. The pet connection will also present opportunities to meet other pet owners. Dogs, in particular, will take you outside, where, when walking with your pet, you will find many instances where you can strike up a conversation. Be sure to inquire if there is a local dog park in your area.

75. Look for Possibilities and Expect Success

After a major loss, searching for possibilities in the present and for your future life is a function of hope. Hope is seldom addressed as a critical part of coping well with any loss. However, examining any problem associated with your loss and listing the possibilities for dealing with it is sound thinking—hope in action. Anything is possible. You can get good friends to brainstorm with you and come up with even more possible ways to solve a problem or create something useful. There is considerable research showing that higher levels of hope are associated with greater success in managing life problems. Make every effort to widen your range of choices and resources as you frame your expectations and start the reconstruction of life without your loved one.

Establish Successful Habits

Review your skills and abilities. What do you do well? Get back to doing it as soon as possible. This will affect the way you feel about yourself, and in the process you will be adding something good to strengthen your inner life. Successful habits will lift you and your spirit, reframe the way you see your life, and help you realize that you are gaining on the transition that has to be faced. Success is commonly built on a bunch of failures. Use them wisely in planning your next move forward. No one is perfect. Think in terms of "failing toward your goal" of reinvesting in life.

Think in Terms of Possibilities

It is critical to understand and believe that there are always options in whatever problem you must face due to your great loss. What is the difference between options and possibilities? Options are clear choices you have already thought about that you may or may not like. Possibilities are where your imagination and inquiries of others come in to brainstorm the thinkable and the unthinkable. So look at the obvious options, and then use your creative thinking to design possibilities you have yet to try.

There are always more out there. The possibilities you discover can now be turned into options, the central core of growing through your dark night.

76. Be Aware of Previous Losses Adding to Your Current Loss

It is not unusual for past losses to bring painful memories that may or may not add to your existing sadness with your current loss. Do not allow these memories to imply that you are weak or that you should never be thinking of the past at a time like this. Once again, this is another common adjunct to normal grieving, and you can allow these recollections to pass out of your thoughts as easily as they came in. There is a big difference between remembering the past and living in the past.

Previous losses have a way of resurfacing each time we have to grieve a new loss. This is especially true when other losses have occurred recently. But it can be equally devastating if the loss took place years ago and you never had the chance to finish unfinished business or say goodbye, or were either left out or unable to attend services for the deceased.

If you have been getting flashbacks of previous losses and the feelings of additional sadness they bring, it may be necessary to go back to the previous loss and come to grips with the source of your pain. You can do this by way of someone you trust implicitly with your feelings about the past. Describe what specifically has come back to you and is adding to the sadness of your recent loss. Ask for an opinion on how your confidant would deal with it if he or she was faced with the problem. If that does not seem to help, do not hesitate to get a professional opinion on a course of action you can take. There are many ways to deal with unresolved past losses that only a trained counselor can suggest.

Most importantly: deal with one loss at a time. No two losses are exactly the same, and therefore each needs to be processed individually. In the case of multiple losses, start with the one that is easiest to talk about. When that has been thoroughly explored, move to the next easiest to talk about. If they are all difficult to think and talk about, start with the one that feels the most urgent or is giving you the most distress.

77. Treat Your Grief as a Multi-Dimensional Response

Grief is a whole-person response, not simply the emotional reaction that is emphasized by the culture in which you live. Everything is affected, and we can counter the excessive negative effects by examining five characteristics and addressing each of them as they demand. Try this approach at various times throughout the day when you grow weary of your grief and the bombardment of anguish and pain. Evaluate yourself, choose a priority, and make a move. All successful problem-solving, and yes, coping well, starts with a question. Here are five questions to move on that I ask mourners to think about and act on to achieve what they want at this particular time.

What Do You Want Psychologically?

Consider your emotional state and what particular emotion is causing pain. Are you feeling all alone? Who or what can assuage the hurt? Whom can you contact and have a conversation with? Can you engage in a project or chore? Do you need a hug or someone to say, "I love you"? Who will show compassion and caring for others that will change your focus? Do you need to look at life differently?

What Do You Want Physically?

Consider the need for a relaxation release technique (like EFT), a temperature change, a walk out of doors, a particular type of food, or a warm bath. What specific behavior could you add or avoid to meet your needs?

What Do You Want Socially?

Consider if you are reaching out enough to interact with others. Or do you need time alone, to get away from all of the attention? Should you go somewhere to be around people you do not know, like at the local mall or library? Should you call a friend and ask if she will go with you to shop or have a cup of tea? As you can see, our emotional state is closely aligned to our social relationships.

What Do You Want Spiritually?

Consider doing some spiritual reading, attending a concert, talking to a spiritual person, or if you believe in God, praying to Him or your loved one for wisdom to adapt. Do you need to spend more time on developing your spiritual life, or are you taking it for granted?

What Do You Want Cognitively?

Are you hurting because you do not feel you are understood? Do you need someone who thinks along the lines of your values and needs? Perhaps you need input about grief and what to expect from an expert on the subject. Or do you need to find someone to talk about your intellectual interests as a diversion for this particular day? True inner peace comes through focused attention and an awareness of the need to release anxiety-producing thoughts affecting your body.

To take advantage of the five self-evaluation questions, you have to be willing to change the way you think. These questions are the basis for identifying the specific goal and the action you must take to achieve it. Make a list of the actions and go for them.

78. Recognize the Gain Associated with Your Loss

Loss and gain are inextricably combined. Consider the possible gains that have come due to your great loss. Those gains may not be immediate or easily identified. You may have to allow time and experience to bring the recognition of gain to your attention. This in no way means that you are minimizing the death of your loved one or trivializing the anguish and sorrow you are experiencing. Nonetheless, there are gains that occur which may help you find some semblance of meaning in the death of your loved one and help in adapting to your loss.

For example, what gains have occurred that are associated with the death of my infant daughter? As a counselor, I have been able to better understand the behavior and respect the deep sorrow of others who have lost a child. I also know that when mourners who have lost a child find out that I have gone through a similar experience, they are much more open and connect with me. A more authentic presence seems to pervade our relationships.

Does this mean I more fully accept what happened to Karen so long ago? Not at all. However, it does give me a greater sense of perspective on life and death and how everything seems to be connected. Life is so much more precious than I had earlier realized. Finding some gain in your great loss may well help you cope with it on a deeper unconscious level and change your perspective about the meaning of life on a conscious level.

79. Recognize and Accept the Role of Anticipatory Grief

Are you wondering why the intensity of your grief is less than expected? Or are you wondering why you may be experiencing moments of relief? The after-death grief response is highly individual—and is sometimes influenced by our anticipatory grieving.

Anticipatory grief involves mourning losses in the past and the present, as well as in the future *before* your loved one died. This means that if your loved one died after a long illness or period of debilitation, you have probably been grieving long before your loved one actually died. For example, it is common to feel sad and grieve when, early in an illness, it is obvious that your loved one can no longer do some of the things he liked to do, which may have included travel, a hobby, or regularly giving assistance to others. Your grief may have been further centered on the way your relationship had to change when the loved one was no longer able go bowling with you or walk in the park as you had for years.

Each day, you experienced additional changes when his health deteriorated further, his independence slipped away, and his role in the family changed dramatically. And then you may have thought of the additional losses that were to come and the impending death. Your anticipatory grief may also have reached well into the future as you thought of what you were going to do without him. All of this grieving and the many issues that have to be dealt with (for example, separation anxiety, bargaining, the pain your loved one is experiencing, etc.) occur before the actual death, yet you still mourn and can be fully involved with your loved one.

While it is quite normal to grieve strongly *before* your loved one died, there is always the possibility that there may have been premature detachment or an emotional pulling away. If this occurred, and you now feel guilty as you look back, it is important to deal with your guilt with a professional counselor or close friend.

However, keep in mind that many people mourn for a long time before the death and are able to accept the eventual death in a less intense way. Thus the nature of their after-death grief may pose a problem for their expectations. Others are not affected by their previous anticipatory grieving. They grieve intensely once their loved one has died.. There is no right or wrong here, only what is right for you. Accept your feelings as intimately connected to all you have been through before the death and all of the grief you have already experienced. There is nothing wrong with not meeting expectations, yours or those of anyone in your family.

80. Visit the Cemetery or Place of Disposal

"Should I 'visit' the loved one?" is a thought entertained by many mourners. Visiting the cemetery or memorial garden can be a help to your grief work or a hindrance. Is it a priority for you? In order to find out, try making a visit, either alone or with a friend if you harbor any fear associated with going there. It may be helpful for you, early in your grief, to go and "talk" to your loved one, say a prayer, or just be silently present. After the visit, assess how you feel. What insights have you derived from the visit, if any? You may need to stay away for a while or return frequently. Again, this is all individual, and there are no set rules, nor are you obligated to go if you choose not to.

On the other hand, you could be spending too much time there. Ask yourself whether it is affecting your acceptance of the death. If you are taking time away from other duties at home or work, reconsider your schedule of visits. If you initially visit frequently and then begin to decrease the number of times you go to the gravesite, this is a normal and common occurrence.

You may feel sad if your loved one was buried a long distance away or out of state and you cannot visit. Yet this does not mean you are forgetting him by not visiting. My parents, brother, and sister are buried fifteen hundred miles from where I live. Every other year, when I go back up north, I always make it a ritual to visit their graves. For me, it is another way to love in separation by honoring their memory.

If you are unable to make a visit, do not put yourself down. Find another way to honor the loved one on special days. Or think about substituting a special place that you can visit as a meaningful sign of your love for the deceased. Some people have a corner in their garden or on a nearby piece of land that they own, even a place they used to go with the loved one. The pivotal question to think about is "Do the visits help me with my grief?" If you feel it doesn't help, it's okay not to visit.

81. Overcome the Constant Sense of Loneliness

Everyone has bouts of loneliness, whether young or old; it is a pervasive experience throughout life. Most loneliness is created by the way we perceive the situation we find ourselves in.

Widows and widowers know all too well the pangs of loneliness when they are living alone. What can be done to deal with the inevitable? Here is what we know is most helpful:

- First, identify the intensity and type of loneliness you must deal with. There are three basic forms of loneliness: cognitive (you have specific interests in subjects but no one to share and discuss them with), behavioral (you lack companionship for eating out, shopping, going to museums, the movies, or other social events), and emotional (your basic need to feel loved and convinced that someone really cares is not being met).

Emotional and behavioral isolation are frequent in the lives of mourners.

- Become aware of the basic solution to loneliness agreed upon by most loneliness experts: self-development. That is, begin the project of developing a better relationship with yourself. This means evaluating your skills, abilities, and desires. Plan on developing new skills, if needed, or fine-tuning old ones. Develop new interests. Decide what you can do to become more involved in the community in which you live.

- Build a social network and increase the quality of your social skills (see **#100, Develop Your Social Skills**) and your ability to interact with others. Learn the art of being approachable. Increase the knowledge base around your main interests. Self-knowledge is at the core of emotional resilience and dealing with the new life you are forging.

- Realize that your loneliness is, like your grief, one of a kind. It is an ongoing condition that depends on your active involvement and recognition of what specific individual needs are not being met. The solution then will be an individual one just for you.

- Become an expert on delivering the four A's: to be given sincere *attention*, to be *accepted*, to be *appreciated*, and to receive *affection*. Everyone wants the four A's at the right time, and delivered by the right person. Take the time to consider specific behaviors that demonstrate these four needs. For example, ask yourself how you can give attention to others. Calling them by name, complimenting them on an item of clothing, sending a card, or telephoning are good beginnings. Take each of the four A's and build lists of how you can deliver each.

- Start today to develop what may be the most important social skill you can possess: validation. It is another universal need that makes us feel important, connected, and appreciated by the other person. "The deepest principle of human nature," said William James, the father of modern psychology, "is the craving to be appreciated." Validating with sincere feeling generates the fulfillment of this great need in others.

- Think of the words of others that have validated and inspired you the most. Become an expert at connecting with others on a *feelings level*, being adept at mirroring joy or worry, delight or anguish, happiness or sadness, and a host of other emotions. Then you will have found the most powerful mechanism for establishing meaningful relationships and your hedge against loneliness.

- Create a pattern of caring routine. This could involve people, pets, plants (growing vegetables in planters on your back porch), yourself, or the environment (one woman in one of my support groups found great pleasure in pulling weeds around her house). True caring for someone or something in your life will keep loneliness at bay.

Examine the following four areas and how you can expand them in your life.

▸ 1. Make a list of the solo activities you enjoyed when your loved one was alive. What can you now add to it?

▸ 2. Review the human contact you have each day and what you need to do to increase the number of contacts.

▸ 3. Think of the shared tasks or mutual projects that you could become involved in at the community level.

▸ 4. Consider breakthroughs—doing things you have never done before. For example, going out to eat alone, buying a season ticket to a local playhouse, going on an Elderhostel trip, or hosting a group of friends.

SIX

Little-Used But Highly Effective Healing Strategies

Believe nothing, no matter where you read it, or who said it, no matter if I have said it, unless it agrees with your own reason and your own common sense.

—BUDDHA

Buddha's quote applies to this entire book or any book on grief that you read, but especially for the strategies that follow. Many of the coping strategies in this final section can be useful in the present moment and long into the future. How you choose to apply them to your present loss—as well as to some of the additional losses that are bound to come as you age—will make a major impact on the quality of your life. Equally important, consistently employed, they will affect your aging process for the better.

82. Be Open to New Ideas, Assumptions, and Beliefs

No one knows why we are given these great losses when we are so unprepared to deal with them. Major losses always have lasting effects, because they jar our awareness so we can expand our spiritual selves. Whatever you do, don't miss the opportunity that your trials and tribulations offer. Although we are vulnerable when deeply grieving, it is also a time when new perceptions of the world are born. It is a mystery how, through the days and months of sorrow, we develop a greater awareness of life, the self, our beliefs, and why we are here.

So many people say that their loss and subsequent grief has brought new insight and appreciation of so much more than they had previously realized. Commit to be open to a bigger picture, to receive new wisdom and understandings that are sure to bring you deeper meaning and mystery. If you want to grieve, cope, and age well, grow intellectually, emotionally, and spiritually.

The Open-Minded Attitude

Are you open to changing beliefs and assumptions (such as "after all, it has been six months, and I still have bad days") that are complicating your grief? This restructuring, though painful, may even affect your values and will open new options in long-term adjustment. Do you have rigid guidelines for how you must hide feelings or relate to others, drummed into you by well-meaning adults? Reread the earlier section on the power of beliefs: you know they affect everything you do in life, especially the way you manage inevitable change.

All of this points to the need to be open to trying new ideas and behaviors that you glean from reliable sources. Flexible thinking styles have long been associated with a reduction in stress. Modeling what has worked for many others is a great coping response. But it demands your openness to try. For most, there is a lot to learn, especially in how to accept impermanence. Have you accepted unpredictability as part of life, grief, and the process of transformation? Step back; look for what you can learn from this great change in life. Have you become more sensitive to the sufferings of others?

Big, life-changing events also routinely cause us to examine the direction of our lives and try never-used approaches. It is not uncommon for what was important before to now seem insignificant. Often, new imaginative insights program healing, leading to optimal wellness. Keep in mind something that I need to repeat, and that few people consistently put into practice: your mind-set has constant powerful physical consequences on your health, vitality, and the emotional fitness you will carry through the rest of your life.

In reality, loss is a great teacher of the importance of relationships, humility, and gratitude. Allow your inner wisdom to help you become aware of alternative ways of looking at the world. Take a moment to think of the beliefs you hold concerning your loss. Are they fair or unfair? Dysfunctional? What do you believe about listening, speaking about feelings, seeking the support of others, and dealing with the terrible bleakness of being isolated and feeling as though no one understands? In your openness lies the power to reflect on and better know yourself.

Beliefs that Make a Difference

Returning to the power of beliefs, here are six that have helped millions of people through the grief process. Think about shaping these beliefs to your value system. They have been proven again and again to be positive bridges to transformation.

- **Believe that love lives on**. Although the physical relationship has ended, love never dies. Love and the person's spirit are always present if you simply look into your heart or quietly sit and use the gift of your inner silence. Meditation will help here. He or she is only a thought away. We are all connected to each other. *Be open to the wonder of the unseen.* If you have doubts, read and talk to others who believe and have experienced the unknown or have had mystical experiences.

- **Believe your pain will lessen**. Pain does diminish; it is one of the major characteristics of grief. The human body cannot hold the pain of grief forever. Most mourners do not feel the same intensity of pain from their grief after the first year. You may not believe it at this time, but let the flame of hope stay alive. No one knows when it will happen, but it always does. Your pain will lose its edge, though it will not be totally eliminated. You will outlast it and be stronger for it. Yes, down the road it may revisit. Then you can let it work through you again and let it go.

- **Believe there is a higher power who will not quit on you.** There is a long history of this belief throughout the ages. Ask and seek this help as others have; it is a hidden treasure. Know that you will be heard. Believe you are on a divinely guided journey, a spiritual being in a physical universe. Believe you will receive what is needed to adapt to your loss, if you ask.

- **Believe that failure is a form of learning**. You will see yourself as having fallen behind at times. Grief is like that, with its failing moments. Don't get down on yourself. You are bound to make mistakes, forget something, or miss an appointment. These miscues do not make you a failure; they make you a learner. Grief is part of a full life in which bright ideas and best-laid plans often go astray. Accept the likelihood of slipups as instructive; decide on the cause, and the cure. Commit to being a successful failure. Don't allow yourself to be jaded with fear of a repeat: let the situations go and restart. See yourself doing better, with a specific strategy, at the next opportunity.

- **Believe in giving your all.** Give 100 percent in what you seek to achieve each day. Achievement leads to more motivation. Observe the universal law: only honest effort leads to success, and only through effort will you face the pain of change and reinvest in life. There is no free lunch. You must do it all, and not in a half-hearted manner. Giving your best effort will result in who you become and how you cope. And this action will positively change your thought life.

- **Believe that your thoughts have the power to heal**. A belief is a repetitive thought. Never forget: *belief has the power to heal*, as proven by the placebo effect. Think healing: "I'm going to get better." Now you are implanting the belief in your unconscious mind. In doing so, you will be installing a new program and pushing out the old. Remember, we have to discard inflexible, indoctrinated beliefs that cause pain. That is another of your choices.

Muster the courage to go where you have never been when the thought presents itself. You have it in you; it is a decision you can make. The French author Anaïs Nin couldn't have said it better when she wrote, "Life shrinks or expands in proportion to one's courage." That courage is based on self-belief. Believe you will heal and it will happen.

83. Trust Mystery and the Unknown

Life is full of mystery that science cannot begin to explain. Despite the many factors which encourage the secularization of life, by no means has the scientific community been able to define the limits of the possible. Of course, there is a strong tendency to reject that which we don't understand. Yet trusting in the mysteries of life has always been a major resource for developing possibilities and inspiration to adapt to change. It is a tool anyone can use. "We have to realize," said English scientist

David Darling in *Soul Search*, "that there are some truths that transcend rationality, that lose their essence if we push too hard for explanations and discussion." Put another way, the truths of mystery and the unknown are happening all the time, and are real to the person experiencing them.

Millions of mourners have reported extraordinary experiences (EEs) after the death of their loved ones. They are convinced a sign or message has been given to them by the deceased, angels, or a supreme being. Many pray for a sign. They *know* there are physical forces in the universe other than those recognized by science, as well as a world of the spirit. This form of human communication, the comingling of two worlds, has occurred continuously throughout history and will obviously happen again and again. These mysterious encounters invariably bring comfort and peace, as recipients believe their loved ones and/or the divine are actively participating in their grief work.

Extraordinary experiences exceed the knowledge we have of causation. EEs possess two characteristics, according to those who report them: they are spontaneous in nature, not invoked, and they appear to come from an outside source. They occur at various times after the death. EEs include sensing the presence, feeling a touch, hearing the voice, or smelling an odor associated with the deceased, as well as a host of synchronistic, third-party, and symbolic events. Here is an example.

> My name is Julie Wojtisek, and on August 3, 2007, my twenty-two-year-old grandson died of an accidental

overdose of prescription drugs. He was found dead in his apartment while attending the University of Tulsa. Two months prior to Jimmy's death I also lost my husband of fifty-eight years to lung cancer. I went to Florida to be with my daughter and was there for most of the winter. In April [2008] I left my daughter Kathy's home to spend a week with my son, who also lives in Florida. On the first night I was there I went to bed at my usual time at around 10:00, and at 4:00 a.m. I woke up and was surprised at the time, as I usually wake up about every hour. Upon waking I went to the bathroom, and when I came back to my bedroom I left the door slightly open so that I could see when my son got up, because I was certain I would not go back to sleep again. I lay down and after just a few minutes I turned to the other side, and there at the foot of my bed was Jimmy. I pulled myself up and said "Jimmy…is that you?" and I'm not sure if he said yes or just nodded his head, but whatever it was, he then vanished, and as he did, the door to my bedroom slammed with great force. Needless to say, I never did go back to sleep and I just couldn't wait to call my daughter Kathy. People will say to me that I was probably just dreaming, but one thing I know for sure is that this was not a dream. From that day on, not only me but my daughter and her husband all did so much better. I don't know why I was selected but felt very honored that I was chosen and that I am able to let others know that Jimmy lives on and obviously appeared to me so that I could reassure others that there is life after death.

The following is Jimmy's mother Kathy speaking:

I go to bed very early and usually sleep soundly until about 4:00 a.m., but on the night of Jimmy's death I went to bed around 9:00 and awoke one hour later with a horrible nightmare. I was standing on a narrow path and I was surrounded by water on all sides, and out of the water came all these horrible demons with fire coming out of their mouths, but I remember thinking…I'm safe…they can't hurt me. This dream startled me so that I couldn't go back to sleep, and for some reason I knew that something had happened to Jimmy. I started calling him and I never stopped all night. In the morning I was sobbing and told my husband that I knew something had happened to him, and Jim said, "Why do you think that?" I told him about my dream and that I called Jimmy all night with no answer. He, of course, said that I know how Jimmy leaves his phone in the car or doesn't charge it, etc., etc. After about an hour of my hysterics I convinced Jim to call the campus and they went in and found him. All I can make of this dream is that Jimmy, from the age of about fourteen, suffered from severe anxiety and was on Xanax (which was what he overdosed on). I believe that he was tortured by demons and that he was finally safe. That is what I got from that dream. Incidentally, the coroner's report stated that his time of death was approximately 10:00 that evening.

We loved our son as much as any parent could have loved a child. I said to Jimmy more than once, "Oh, please be careful, because if anything ever happened to you, I don't think your dad and I could ever survive." I believe he knew he had to come back…he was right, and we are surviving as a result of my mother's visit with Jimmy. I know he is waiting for us and just wanted to give us some peace in the meantime.

Premonitions like Kathy's have occurred to many others before the death of a loved one, as it did to my wife before the death of our daughter. The key question that presents itself to the mourner is, "Now that your loved one has demonstrated she or he lives on and will always care, what are you going to do to start accepting the challenge of change and the reality of the loss?"

Believing Is Seeing

I once had a physician contact me about an EE she had after the death of her father. After agreeing that it was an authentic experience, she followed up with these comments: "Thank you for helping me see that, just because I can't explain it scientifically, does not make it any less real. I know what I felt, saw, and heard and I am a different person because of it. Thank you for that affirmation." This from a person who has been highly trained in the scientific method *not* to believe in anything that cannot be seen, weighed, or measured. As Carl Jung wrote, "Physical is not the only criterion for truth: there are also psychic truths which can neither be explained nor proved nor contested in any physical way." What you have been taught to see at this point in life is based largely on what you were taught to believe. Jung suggests looking at life through an uncommon lens that brings peace from chaos.

Look for and expect mystery in your grief work. Believe that there is a reason mystery and the unknown exist. Use the emotional energy generated to meet the changes that must be faced. When you receive one of these gifts, the message is: you are loved, you have been given to, so give back, and make giving a priority each day. This is the message of mystery.

If you so believe, pray for an assist from the unknown, as unscientific as that sounds. Expect unexpected help. It will come and surprise you. Your loved one is concerned about you, wants you to know that she knows what you are going through, and will do whatever it takes to ease your burden. Your loved one expects the relationship to continue, not in the same way as in the past, but in a way that you must learn. You are always loved.

EEs reflect peace, joy, and ongoing relationships. In short, they are love lessons. Deceased loved ones are there to help and give support. They want you to know there will be a reunion. Millions have been helped by their experiences and see the world from a whole different perspective as a result. Read about these fascinating experiences that have been turning points in the grief of others. See the reading list at the end of the book.

84. Ask for a Visitation Dream or a "Sign"

A woman I know described how her brother coped with the death of both of their parents:

> My brother described his grief as being like a "pain in your knee"—it hurt all of the time, but you learn to walk with it. He said he had a very short fuse and was angry about being angry all the time. He wrote music and poetry. He planted two memorial trees for our parents and has coffee with them once in a while. He talks to them and asks them to visit in a dream, and they do. He sees little mannerisms in his young girls that remind him of our parents. He was lucky enough to have a spouse who would listen to his rants and hold him when he cried.

The preceding illustrates two important points: her brother had employed several ways to deal with the death of his parents, and was open to talking with them and asking them for a dream visitation. Each night during REM sleep, about an hour and a half, we dream. Dreams provide much information about feelings, relationships, and needed behavior through the symbols they create and the insights that evolve.

Millions of people who are mourning the death of a loved one have reported receiving a dream visitation from their deceased loved one or a divine being. All of these contacts are comforting and are great sources of meaning to survivors.

You can use your dreams to help you cope with the death of your loved one. Here is a common approach for seeking a visitation dream used by many mourners:

- Try to relax and facilitate sleep by thinking of some loving memories from when your loved one was alive. Take some deep breaths and focus on the comforting images you have created. Go over the scene in detail, the time of day, place, weather, what was said, who else was there, and the conversation. After a few minutes, repeat the word "peace" or "sleep" each time you exhale, and try to go off to sleep.

- Counselors who are open to the EE phenomena often suggest that the mourner pray for an encouraging sign that his or her loved one is okay. Each evening before you retire, ask God or your higher power to allow you to have a comforting dream visit from your loved one. And ask for protection from unwanted dreams or dream figures. Be patient and have faith in God or your higher power to hear your petition.

- Keep a dream journal and record your dream when it occurs. Place a pen and writing pad on the night table by your bed. A true visitation dream is never forgotten; it will be vivid, clear, and insightful. It will be useful to immediately write down all the small details of the dream for later reading. You can use it as a resource for dealing with unwanted thoughts at a later time. It is also a record to pass on to your children or relatives and becomes a part of family history.

- When you receive your dream, give thanks. Remember, most people who are mourning will dream of their loved one, but not all dreams are visitation dreams. A visitation dream possesses a special sense of clarity, meaning, and reality. It will be an extremely positive, unforgettable experience, and you will know you have been given a gift of comfort.

- Listen intently to your dreams. Share them with a knowledgeable person. Be consistent in asking for them as well as for the insight to deal with change, until you receive an answer. You will be awed by what you receive and the bonanza of insights that develop on what you could do to adapt to the new conditions of your life.

85. Determine Your Secondary Losses and Grieve Each of Them

Most people who are grieving are not aware of the impact of numerous secondary losses on the way their grief work is going. Yet all major losses involve secondary losses. Secondary losses may be financial losses, social losses (some friends no longer include you in activities), a loss of companionship, a loss of a source of wise counsel, the loss of a sexual partner, the loss of part of your old life, or the loss of your home due to changes in income.

Often forgotten as secondary losses and bringing much grief is the loss of dreams for the future with the loved one ("We were going to build a home in Florida"). Equally painful is the loss of meaning in life. All of these and more are legitimate sources of loss and deserve to be recognized as individual reasons to grieve.

The key understanding is that each loss be recognized, talked about, and mourned as an individual loss. But take it slow, and deal with one loss at a time. Gradually assess where you are in dealing with your loss and how the secondary loss comes into play. Some of these secondary losses may appear months or years later, such as when a grandchild graduates from high school or college or a child is born, and the deceased is not there. For many, the sadness at these events is deeply felt, and it's okay to cry or express your sadness at this time.

86. Maintain Your Brain

Grief not only affects emotions but especially affects brain function. Sadness, focusing on negative memories, and the activation of pain centers in the brain add to the stress and confusion that commonly accompany the process of recovery. Your brain affects everything you do—physiologically, mentally, behaviorally, and spiritually.

In addition, it is not uncommon for mourners to eat little, lose sleep, and often drink too much coffee or alcohol. Many physicians agree that the resulting chronic dehydration adds to the hastening of degenerative diseases and a massive assault on the brain and its important functions. The final, and arguably among the most damaging, assaults come if you smoke, which is a major factor in reducing cognitive functioning.

Here is what you can do for brain health as you grieve and help yourself move toward healing with good judgment, more vigor, less physical pain, and limited confusion:

- Eat protein at least three times daily, preferably at breakfast, lunch, and dinner (especially breakfast), since this is major brain fuel. Protein contains an amino acid (tyrosine) that increases the levels of norepinephrine and dopamine, important neurotransmitters in the brain. Your body can't store protein; you need to consume it daily.

- Start eating an omega-3 rich diet, such as wild salmon or fish oil supplements (krill oil is even better), to assist cerebral circulation and, equally important, help your heart as well as reduce inflammation in the body. The brain cannot function without omega-3s. They will reduce much physical pain as you grieve. Also, load up on antioxidants (vitamins E and C, and beta-carotene), which will fight free radicals that damage brain cells.

- Eliminate toxins from your diet, such as those found in artificial sweeteners like high fructose corn syrup, which is in most everything you can imagine (a bit of an exaggeration, but just read labels and you will be surprised). Also, remove crystalline fructose and aspartame. Soda is a huge culprit here.

- Again, here comes the importance of daily exercise in order to increase blood flow and nutrition to the brain. Exercise stimulates nerve growth (neurons and connections between neurons) and increases the neurotransmitter dopamine. But there is more: exercise has been shown to increase memory and cognitive function. You can keep your brain young. Significantly, exercise will give you an energy lift because of the mental stimulation resulting from the release of hormones into the blood.

- Aromatherapy is often looked on as a meaningless waste of time and money. Not so! According to neuroscientists, certain smells can stimulate the brain and affect moods. Not only does the use of essential oils like peppermint, lemon, lavender, hazelnut, almond, orange, or cypress enhance moods, but some oils can induce relaxation and improve sleep. I often spray lavender on my pillow before retiring. Never use essential oils on the skin undiluted; many of these oils are dangerous if ingested.

- Hydrate. For brain health alone—remember that 80 percent of the brain consists of water—drink more clean spring water daily than whatever is your normal beverage is a must. It will ease your pain. Start sipping water as soon as you get to the kitchen (I drink eight ounces first thing in the morning, every morning) before you put on the coffee or start making your meal. Even a few ounces will be helpful as a starter.

- Most important: If you are a smoker, whatever you do at this time of great stress, don't increase the number of times you smoke. Smoking is the worst thing you can do to your brain, especially when mourning. Why? It causes irritation and inflammation—the predecessors of illness. If at all possible, cut back and eventually eliminate this vicious brain-cell killer.

- Avoid conflict as much as possible, as well as sources of negativity. Put another way, pick your disagreements with others carefully. Is it really worth the hassle to argue a particular point? Stress increases inflammatory conditions within the body.

- Cognitive challenges are brain-healthy challenges: keep involved. Be willing to go to new places with your life. You will regain a sense of fulfillment if you find something you love to do.

- Increase brain-cell connections by learning new ways of dealing with loss. Also, try new activities to develop a variety of interests, which not only will help your brain increase connections but are also critical in the process and challenge of adapting to loss and change.

Bottom line: Consider all of the preceding as coping techniques that will help you do your grief work and manage pain.

87. Intentionally Establish a New Relationship with Your Deceased Loved One

Establishing a new relationship with the deceased is another important goal of grieving that is infrequently addressed. That is why earlier in your reading I have often made reference to it. Most grief experts consider a new relationship to be a high point on any mourner's task list. Although eventually your loved one will not be the centerpiece of each day, you will always have a relationship with him or her. It is an ongoing cognitive process based on the memories and traditions of the past and your shared life. It is especially important to balance traditions with new changes and develop a strong, positive memory relationship. Thus, you can always celebrate a life that has been lived, lessons learned, and legacies left.

Plan on recognizing birthdays, seasonal events, and anniversaries of the deceased, inwardly and/or outwardly. Include remembrances at holidays and family gatherings, if you so desire. Speak to your loved one whenever you see fit, as millions of others before you have done (see **#55, Speak to Your Loved One**). All of this must be accomplished in concert with efforts to keep an honest memory of the deceased, recognizing that no one is perfect. Idealizing the loved one can make it more difficult for you to accept the death, and you are likely to alienate other family members as well.

On the other hand, believing the loved one is with you in spirit each day is a motivating force for many.

88. Build a Data Bank of Gratitude Memories

One of the greatest secrets of the good life is *wanting what we already have*. Gratitude memories are among the most powerful road maps to a peaceful mind-set that we already possess. Each one of us has a number of stored happy memories and experiences. More importantly, they continue to happen each day, even though we are grieving and are not looking for them. We simply overlook them in our sorrow. Gratitude memories have an especially powerful positive effect on shifting perspective, affecting the brain, and changing physical feelings. Focusing on them draws more to be grateful for into our lives as it pushes out anxiety.

Carefully look at what you have—people, experiences, life, and things—and look for something to express gratitude for every day. Why establish the habit of accumulating and frequently reviewing gratitude memories at a time of sorrow? It is a foolproof way to affect your inner life for the better, right now and *for the rest of your life*.

You can generate the atmosphere of gratitude by using the standard set-up phrase used in a great therapeutic technique call EFT (see **#18, Consider Learning EFT**). It goes like this "Even though I [am suffering, feel sad, am down, etc.—use the words that feel best for you], I deeply and completely love and accept myself." Now examine your possibilities, your talents, and your past successes. What you have cannot be taken away, unless you fail to recognize the treasure that is yours.

Types of Gratitude Memories

There are two classifications of gratitude memories: daily and lifelong. A practice that can help you immensely is to start listing gratitude memories at the close of each day. Ask yourself what you are thankful for each evening. Your list might include: a difficult task you completed; an old friend who contacted you; a good night's sleep; your cold or allergies cleared up unexpectedly; you had a delicious meal; you realize how many friends love you and help you in times of trouble; you had the energy to get through the day. Consider what went well and got you through a particular hour or over an expected obstacle. Here is a useful approach: "If you concentrate on finding whatever is good in every situation," said Rabbi Harold Kushner, "you will discover that your life will suddenly be filled with gratitude, a feeling that nurtures the soul."

Go to Sleep on Gratitude

Focus on the gratitude memories of the day as you lie in bed each night. Make it a habit to go to sleep on gratitude. These memories will create a relaxing mindset conducive to promoting sleep, especially when you recall being loved. (I often recall this lifelong gratitude memory: the love of my mother for her five children, including a set of twin daughters, and how dedicated she was in making our little lunch sandwiches, putting them in our lunch-boxes, and sending us off to school each day.)

Go with and immerse yourself in the feeling and the implications that accompany your memory. When you wake up in the middle of the night and can't get back to sleep, again invoke gratitude memories of either kind. Think back on these great experiences and those who loved you, and replay the love and circumstances that inspired the people involved. Of course, don't forget your higher power.

Writing gratitude events in a little notebook (create a gratitude journal) to look back on and refresh your memory over the months ahead will be useful, since reprocessing positive memories is an assist in the adjustment process. They are like written affirmations. Read them first thing in the morning; it's a great way to start the day on an upbeat note. Put a gratitude note on your screen saver to set the tone for your work day. Use this approach to block negativity that always wants to creep in, seemingly out of nowhere. Switch on your screen saver.

Keep building on your list each evening (soon it will go into the hundreds), and you will begin to realize you have much that affects your attitude toward life as well as your blood pressure. This presupposes that you develop the habit of noticing when a gift comes to you during the day.

Gratitude awakens awareness of so much that we take for granted as we open to the new possibilities from this hidden treasure. For example, are you thankful for your mobility? This can lead to reframing (developing a different perspective about death and what you still possess) and will alter the way you relate to your great loss and your new life.

Reframes are powerful inner-change agents. As a bereaved mother observed, "It's philosophical, but when I choose to look at his death from a different angle or perspective, it helps me a great deal to understand it all. It seems to make it easier to think about." Others might counter with "What angle could possibly make this easier?" So use the power of your imagination to discover a different perspective, if that feels right for you.

A daily gratitude practice—acting grateful—is another coping skill, a foundation for healing, that you can use for the rest of your life. A great secondary benefit is that you will generate as well as draw more positive energy within and around you. And what most of us forget is this: gratitude eliminates our tendency to complain.

Finally, don't forget to teach your children to practice gratitude each day as you earn it yourself. A simple and sincere "thank you" is a great gratitude starter and a booster shot for interpersonal relationships.

Reviewing your daily gratitude memories will never stop giving good results in ongoing healing. Gratitude energy is a hope-builder, placing you in a higher state of consciousness. The attitude of gratitude soon brings relief, motivation, and the power of choice back into your life more than you ever dreamed possible. Use a word—like "joy," "abundance," "nature," or "love"—that will be your signal to shift into gratitude mode when you spend too much time thinking about what you don't have.

89. Talk to and Listen to Your Body

The nature of your thoughts has a direct effect on biology. Most people do not realize that the mind is so closely integrated with the body. Negative thoughts not only cause deep inner stress and make you sick—they can even cause your demise. Just remember what hostility can do to the heart and circulatory system when allowed to take permanent residence in your thought life.

The exciting news is that your mind plays a major role in changing physical feelings, and physical feelings heavily influence how we think. Stop and listen to your body—the rate of inhaling and exhaling, physical sensations, and heart rate. Next, locate where you feel you store the effects of your emotions, fears, or sadness. Does it feel as though your heart aches? Do you feel it by way of a headache, weakness in the legs, or perhaps an old injury seems to flare up? Then gently accept the sensations and go to work on reducing their intensity.

You can start a new inner program by talking to your body, yes, talking, and visualizing it slowing down and/or revitalizing. For example, every morning before I put my feet on the floor I repeat, fifteen to twenty times, "I am strong," and follow it with "I am having a great day." I visualize a white light going through my body, lighting me up with energy, starting from my toes and following the same path up my body as if I were doing progressive relaxation.

You can visualize yourself successfully going through the day, completing whatever you feel is appropriate, to give you a lift and to inspire. Such self-coaching will have an immediate effect on your body and your day. But you must persist. Start in a small way. Then add additional exercises.

Never, ever forget that your pattern of thinking either creates your optimal physiology or detracts from it. Prove this to yourself by scanning your body and how it feels whenever you think or talk in a negative way or complain about the difficulties you face. You can choose to control physical feelings. You can tell your heart to slow down as you decrease your breathing rate. You can talk to muscles to release tension as you gently stretch them.

While lying in bed, press your lower back gently into the mattress and say, "Stretch and release." Why is this so important? Neuromuscular hypertension (muscle tension) is a product of your emotional health. And you can reverse it and save unneeded suffering. If soreness in a particular muscle, the neck, or ankle signals a storage point for anxiety, gently caress it, talk to it, saying whatever seems appropriate. Start listening to your body for early warnings of distress so you can intervene with a stretch and release movement.

Become more body aware when you eat certain foods. How do you feel after coffee? Hyped up? How do you feel after eating ginger, an apple, or a tomato? Stay alert to what your body is signaling. *You can trust it to tell you what to eat and to stop overeating.* Keeping a food diary can be helpful in your analysis and discovering any food intolerance. Discontinue using any food or supplement you ingest that causes uneasiness or nausea. Most people are completely unaware of how the body influences the brain, its functions, our moods, and emotional disposition. The body and the brain are not separate entities: they are two parts of the same system.

It is clear—how you talk to and treat your body can add immensely in dealing with the stress of grief. Become an expert on reading your body reactions by practicing mindfulness (focused awareness of the moment, which is also an excellent way to deal with unwanted thoughts). Then alter behavior by moving away from or avoiding circumstances that detract from good feelings and energy levels. If you become aware of the power of discernment you possess, your life will never be the same again.

90. Use a Breathing Technique to Intervene in Your Stress Response

One of the most recommended and consistently effective ways to deal with the grief and anxiety of major loss is getting your mind and body to slow down through conscious deep abdominal breathing. Dr. James Gordon, clinical professor of psychiatry at the Georgetown University School of Medicine, says, "Slow deep breathing is probably the single best antistress medicine we have." Specifically, it moves oxygen and lymphatic fluid throughout the body. Practice stillness and quiet by focusing on your breathing to center your reality. The key word here is "practice." You will be able to think more clearly with the increase in oxygen uptake to the brain.

As soon as you recognize your anxiety level rising, sit down, go within, and start breathing slowly. Take *deep* abdominal breaths, where you breathe in through your nose, using a four-count—one thousand one, one thousand two, etc. Fully inflate the lungs (we are all shallow breathers), and let the inhalation push your stomach out slightly, as the diaphragm drops down. Stretch your lungs. Hold for a three-count. Then release the air naturally through your mouth on a four-count (later, increase exhalation to a six-count). Visualize breathing in healing energy (a white light) and tension going out of your body with the exhalation of air. You can use this technique for any situation that you are about to experience that you believe it is going to be difficult to manage. Adjust the counts to what is most comfortable for you after starting with four-three-four.

Practice it when riding in a car or on the bus. If you are alone in your home, close your eyes when you breathe, and focus on the feelings of relaxation as you breathe out. Visualize your fears being exhaled. On each new inhalation, visualize being filled with bright light and energy. Don't expect instant results. Take your time. Locate where you think you are storing the tension.

If you have physical pain or feel the effects of stress on a body part, visualize exhaling *through* that body part. If you feel your heart or chest actually aches, then see your breath going through that area and easing the pain. Repeat several times and at various times throughout the day. You may also want to add this exercise to your solitude time (see **#8, Cultivate a Bit of Solitude for Yourself**) or use it at various times during the day as a mini-break, where you can scan your body for tension.

91. Get a Massage

Don't overlook this one. I have had a number of mourners tell me how comforting and relaxing a massage can be. The healing power of touch (addressed in **#18, Consider Learning EFT**) is a crucial need for all of us; it releases the powerful health-giving neuropeptide oxytocin from the pituitary gland. When you are mourning the death of a loved one, a massage therapist can easily provide this proven stress reducer. Many mourners also experience a strong release of emotions while receiving a massage. An experienced massage therapist expects it, so don't feel silly or bad for crying during the experience. This is a normal healing experience and nothing to be ashamed of regularly scheduling.

There are also some studies that show that for depressed patients, a good massage is as good as antidepressants such as Paxil or Prozac.

Yes, a massage can be expensive, but well worth the cost. If you live in a big city, there may be a massage school in your area that gives free massages from new practitioners who are learning this healthful art. Or you can find a massage therapist who will come to your home. If you are unable to afford a massage, consider a friend or family member who would be willing to give you a shoulder or back massage.

The benefits are many, depending on the type of massage. Emotional and physical stress is reduced through increasing blood circulation and the soothing of tense, anxiety-laden muscles. Massage also assists in the removal of toxins from muscle tissue.

Lymphatic drainage is further enhanced through tissue manipulation. You may also want to consider receiving training in massage as part of developing new interests and skills.

92. See Your Emotions as Inner Messengers

There is another coping strategy that will give you clues on where to take a different direction in the way you are dealing with the absence of your loved one. Examine your emotions in terms of the messages they are sending in the form of questions. Emotions are purposeful and provide great food for thought in changing self-defeating behavior. They are ingenious in that they not only communicate our inner response to change but, equally important, actually provide many messages about how to deal with the current dilemma.

The most obvious emotions associated with grief are anger, guilt, and sadness, which is often mislabeled as depression. Some mourners experience one or more of these emotions, including reactive depression; others, none at all. If you are presently dealing with one of the above, examine the questions these emotions pose for you; they have a purposeful function.

What can the emotion teach you?

It may be asking if you should slow down or consider what is most important in life. Sometimes emotions lead us to spiritual transformation. When the questions become clear, apply your answers by taking specific actions, and see if the course of your grief takes a turn for the better. Here are some of the specific questions:

- Anger is a normal emotion that sends the following messages to carefully listen to: "Am I using my anger to cover up other emotions, like fear, frustration, depression, dependency, or guilt? What do I need to protect? Is anger causing me to refuse to accept the death and prolong my suffering? What do I need to restore in order to let go of my anger? What do I need to take back or reclaim?" Anger can be a motivating force for good. "Is my anger thwarting my ability to love? Am I turning my anger into a grudge by refusing to forgive?" A grudge is the assurance of continued misery.

- Guilt usually asks the following: "Is this feeling neurotic guilt (big guilt feelings but little or no real cause) or true cause-and-effect guilt? Am I acting as though I should have been omnipotent and known better at the time of the supposed misdeed?" Frequently, when looking back on an event leading to guilt, the mourner becomes a second guesser. Guilt also asks, "What do I need to change? To do?" Grief perpetually dictates change. And guilt suggests you can change the way you see the event causing guilt.

- The mood disorder of reactive depression (you relate the

depressed feeling to your loss, feel empty, have physical complaints, etc.) is not only one of the most common emotions experienced, it is also the most investigated. The following questions are addressed to those experiencing acute grief with deep sadness and/or reactive depression: "What must I let go of? What routines, beliefs, approaches, relationships, or old parts of my life do I need to give up? What 'new' parts of life must I accept?" And sadness asks one of the most important questions of all: "What knowledge, skills, abilities, or insights do I need to add to my life? What everyday spirituality will help me transcend my great loss?"

Study the questions carefully. They demand much time and careful analysis. The result will be that you will better direct the course of your grief work and use emotion as a tool of self-understanding. Getting in touch with your intuition and emotions is one of the great gifts of grief.

93. Examine Why You Are Where You Are in Your Grief Work

Pause periodically, as the days and weeks go by, and think about how you have made it as far as you have. One month, maybe two, or a year without your loved one has passed. Consider the thoughts and behaviors that have led to more pain and the things you have done that have brought comfort and accomplishment. What skills have you used? Or what hidden talent have you uncovered that you didn't realize you had? Something has gotten you this far. Was it hope that you were not fully aware of? You see, when you endure, that is one of the sources from which hope springs.

Was your ability to organize an asset? Your commitment? A certain belief? Taking a leap of faith? Knowing you are not alone. Your ability to relate to caregivers? In making this examination, you will see that you have moved forward in comparison to when you started on your journey.

Yes, as you look back it seems to be one big blur of pain. But something has brought you to this point. Clearly identify what you need to keep doing and further develop that helps you deal with change. Make a prioritized list that you will use as a reminder each day. Cope smarter, not harder. Likewise, isolate the parts of your grief work that tend to cause additional suffering, and decide on a course of action that you must take to avoid or minimize the precipitating factors. Keep using whatever it is that helps by employing it at other times and in other circumstances. In short, recognize, highlight, and commit to using the strengths you commonly forget or take for granted. You possess them.

94. Individually Grieve Multiple Losses

How can anyone cope with the death of more than one family member when these deaths occur in a short period of time? What happens to the person who is grieving the death of a loved one, then loses a job and has to move from their home or apartment because of financial conditions? Multiple losses occur more frequently than most people realize, and they often complicate the mourning process.

To begin with, it is important to recognize that we grieve many losses in life other than the death of a loved one. The breakup of any close relationship, divorce, incarceration, geographical relocation, children going off to college, destructive fires, workplace changes, or the loss of family heirlooms can bring strong grief reactions. In some instances, these losses initiate a cascade of emotional responses as strong as those associated with the death of a loved one.

How can you cope with these massive changes when experiencing more than one loss?

- Recognize and accept that in suffering multiple losses you will generally need much more time to sort out feelings and deal with the question of "Why?" Often, the intensity of grief will be stronger, and you will need assistance in examining your needs in dealing with each loss, one at a time.
- Now more than ever it is essential to engage trusted grief companions, people who will stand with you, listening to the pain being experienced and expressed. Much commitment is needed from caregivers who will not reduce their contact with you. Allowing grief to run its course with multiple losses is a gigantic commitment for the caregiver. Again, though mourning, you may have to educate some caregivers not to give up on you.

- Prioritize. Decide which death (or other loss) is causing you the most pain at this particular time, what emotion or emotions are most prevalent, and learn how to deal with them. You may or may not be able to do this with friends and family. It may mean going for professional assistance, which is a wise move to make.

- Establish or return to routines as soon as possible for the stability they tend to put back into life. Be patient with yourself. You cannot expect a speedy resolution of all of the changes to be addressed. There will be some trial-and-error moments, and you will have to sit down and try another avenue of approach when one plan doesn't work. Do not rush yourself. Easier said than done, of course, when you are in pain. But that is why you need people who can be around pain.

- Balance in your life and in grief is an absolute must. And above all, walk, walk, walk. This is where a walking meditation would be useful, as described in **#66, Begin a Twenty-Minute Daily Meditation Period**.

- Be careful of falling into thought traps, like you are being punished for your misdeeds. Get rid of thoughts such as, "I'm getting what I deserve," "I'm unlucky," "I can never deal with it all," or "This is what happens when you don't do the right thing." Such self-recriminations have no basis in fact and only increase unnecessary suffering. They distract from facing the new life that multiple losses dictate. Remember: this line of thinking is self-destructive and takes a major toll on your physical self as well as your emotional well-being. No one has a final answer to the question of why multiple losses occur to many people.

- Keep telling yourself—"I can handle this, as difficult as it seems." It is hell, and ever so painful, but you are a survivor who will use the support and insight of others to adjust and start over. There is nothing odd with the feeling of being overwhelmed. Anyone would be. Keep coaching yourself to persist—it will make a big difference.

- Feelings and thoughts change and new ones will pop into your mind and body over the long haul. Look for ongoing support structures. They could be exceptional friends, a grief support group (many members are dealing with multiple losses), a clergy person, a nurse, or a social worker. The information needed to deal with your particular circumstances is often found in the support group and from the facilitator. Ask for recommendations from hospice volunteers, other mourners, your doctor, or your local hospital if you wish to choose a counselor. The choice is important for the connection and trust you will need from that person. Half the battle is finding the kindred souls who can provide an idea or two that you have yet to hear.

Many people suffer multiple losses and the resulting bereavement overload. Although multiple losses tend to exacerbate the length and intensity of the grief process, breaking down and prioritizing where to begin coping with so many changes (both inner and outer) is the place to start.

It is excruciating and pain-filled work, yet you will gradually succeed in adapting. Keep your inner talk positive: "I am dealing with this, come hell or high water," not "This is too much for me." Allow for a relapse or two, or more, but know that you can outlast these terrible circumstances and get through your demanding ordeal.

95. Use Music to Affect Mood and Feelings

Many individuals use music to deal with bouts of loneliness or to lift their spirits during the day. Even our military in war zones use it to deal with the stress of combat. It is clear that certain forms of music (the type varying for each individual person) affect the brain and our grief work in healthy, positive ways, evoke loving memories, and bring comfort and respite.

There appears to be an increase in brain arousal and mood change when music you like music is played. And it is okay to break sadness with it. It does not have to be a specific kind of music, as in the so-called Mozart effect. Consider playing music the loved one liked to honor him or her and to show love in separation.

Not only thoughts but music affects our energy levels. Some research suggests that inspiring music can reduce pain or boost the effectiveness of a painkiller if you are taking one, as well as help manage stress levels. For many people, their favorite music can put them in an upbeat or inspirational mood. This is due to the release of neurotransmitters (the endorphins) which are natural painkillers. When you begin to feel reactive depression is beginning again, see if your brand of music can reduce its intensity. Even combine it with a walk. This is self-therapy you are entitled to and can benefit from.

Retreat and Reflection

Self-knowledge is a key to dealing with change and the many losses that have to be confronted. Therefore, take a moment to think back about the music that has been soothing for you and your individual taste through the years. Studies show that "your" music, just like laughter, can relax and dilate the inner lining of blood vessels, thus increasing blood flow and inducing relaxation. It will reduce heart rate as you put yourself in a nonthreatening environment, focusing exclusively on the music, and letting it take you away from the stress you are under.

Conversely, loud and/or distasteful music you don't care about does just the opposite, adding to your anxiety and stress levels and depleting energy. Get away from it. Remember stress (distress) brings an inflammatory response in the body.

The right music is as effective for some as prayer, meditation, strong social networks, or taking a rest period for minimizing inflammation. Experiment and find your brand of soothing music to add to your stress break, to use on your daily walk, or to play in the house when you are alone. And don't hesitate to hum or sing along, if you are so moved. It can be a great release for you. Also, use those easy-listening songs that slow your breathing, and ultimately deepen the relaxation response, leading to peaceful moments in your grief work.

96. Determine What Recharges You

Create an uplifting events schedule or what I sometimes call a "balancing list." Whatever recharges you, include one or two of these activities in your daily duties. Think back before your loss and decide what boosted your batteries and gave you that "up" feeling. Research tells us that building on the strengths you had before the loss will provide better and faster healing after the loss. Certainly, in part, it was your loved one. He or she is and always will be in your heart, always with you in a different form. And that person can be a motivator for you.

Use that heart recharge and think of what else is or was uplifting. Could it have been prayer, sailing, a nature walk, nine holes of golf, a favorite song, window shopping, talking to your best friend, or taking care of your garden? Was it your willingness to be open and share your knowledge and strengths with others? It may take days or weeks to realize what truly lifts you up. Reserve time to review the last year of your life and you will discover these things. Take each and, at the appropriate time, insert it into your new life and schedule. Make a priority list and add to it as you discover new or forgotten interests or talents. Recall old interests and events from your youthful years that you might include on the list.

When you start feeling that downward spiral, or if you are using the grieving time strategy (see **#30, Establish Time for Grief and Worry**), at the end of the time, pick out one of the events on your balancing list and go for it. Never forget: it is self-care that you need in your grief work and to recharge your energy stores. I know what works without fail: deciding to be kind to yourself. One way you can do this that will change your energy levels for the better is positive self-talk. Go back to First Words (page 1) and look at some of the statements you can use.

97. Create Something

Everyone possesses the ability to create something useful for self or others. You already have that creative energy within. Creating helps bring meaning back into life. Write a book, a blog, or an article about the lessons you have learned from your experiences. What are the tangible takeaways from what you are going through? There are many websites that are looking for short articles of seven to eight hundred words on various subjects. Check out www.ezinearticles.com, for example. They want articles on business, health, nutrition, automobiles, relationships, and politics, to name a few.

Whatever you create is an extension of you that can help restore interest in life. If you are skilled with your hands, build something, draw, or paint a picture. If you have information, a recipe, a strategy for releasing stress, get it out on the Internet and use it to initiate discussions. Consider starting a special interest group.

Have a reason and intention for your creation to give you direction and a way to explore. This activity can lead to a whole new dimension of living. Never confuse creating something with keeping busy. Creating with intention will energize you, if you limit doubt or disbelief from blocking your path. By the same token, creating provides an uplifting spiritual boost.

98. Return to Your Purpose and Passion in Life

Before the death of your loved one, what did you love doing? Your work? Your art? Sharing a skill? Living a commitment? What? The sooner you can reconnect to purpose—or find a new one—you can better integrate your great loss into life. If life is constantly meaningless, you've lost touch with your purpose, your passion, and in some instances your value system. You are still needed and loved. Having a passion again will get you through this nightmare. We all need confirmation of our value, especially when mourning, and we can get it through what we become excited about. Work on getting a passion or. As one mourner said, "I had to get a life."

Purpose = Hope and Power

If you don't have a clear mission or purpose, regardless of your age, now is the important time to craft one. When we are on task, we find our individual meaning. Ask yourself what your strengths are and why you think you are here. Are you doing what you are in the world to do? If not, start a quest for using your insights and abilities to do something you believe is important for a better world, for a better you. You have something to offer humanity that no one else has, even if you have been programmed to believe you don't. You have a talent, something you do better than others do. Review the achievements in your life and what you can add to them.

Worthy purpose will not only give you life again; it is the cornerstone of true joy. Or, as many psychologists say, it is a decision we make. Think carefully about the implications of that last sentence. Consider deciding to carry on a project started by your loved one. As long as you are alive, believe you have a purpose; it takes away pain. You are not here by chance.

How might the search commence? Ask yourself how you would like to be a contribution. Carl Menninger put it this way: "The central purpose of each life should be to dilute the misery in the world." Who can use your wisdom and experience?

To rediscover purpose, think of who or what inspired you before your great loss. Whom do you admire? Who are you thankful for? What needs to be accomplished in your community or regionally? How can you make a difference in someone else's life? Let your voice and actions be heard. How do you want to make something better? Purpose brings peace. Build your day around your purpose.

Start setting some mission goals and make the detailed plans to reach them. Write them down and place them in a spot so that you look them square in the eye every day, and do something about them. Place Friedrich Nietzsche's motto next to them: "He who has a *why* to live can bear almost any *how*." Even though your life has changed, you still have a mission here, your own special purpose. Let your faith in it keep you from letting hopelessness reign.

99. Start a Personal Improvement Project: The Intentional Appreciation of Beauty

In essence, the intentional appreciation of beauty is one of the most important spiritual activities you can develop. While many people, mourners included, see and recognize beautiful things that come into and out of their lives, relatively few set out to intentionally look for beauty each day and incorporate it into their lifestyle. If they did, it would become the basis for a vibrant inner life and ultimately valuing the awe that surrounds them.

Beauty is everywhere, not merely in nature. And yes, even though we all know it is in the eye of the beholder, that is what gives us our individual pathways to seeking what is beautiful for us. First, identify the beauty in your thoughts and wishes. Do you see beauty in babies, trees, paintings, buildings, people, songs, farms, orchards, automobiles, mountains, dancing, sculpture, a smile, rugs, ceramics, and more? Get in touch with that which stirs the soul. Schedule time each day to focus on beauty as a coping response.

Try This Exercise

For the next three minutes, look first for beauty in everything your eyes see. Note the feelings and thoughts that predominate in your three-minute beauty search. What does it do to you inside? Compare the experience with other parts of your day. As time permits, increase your opportunities to look for beauty during different hours of the day and night. Build the practice into one of your new routines in the months and years ahead. In doing so you will discover a healing remedy, or as G. K. Chesterton, the English author, observed, "There is a road from the eye to the heart that does not go through the intellect." Once on that road, you will have reinvested in life.

100. Develop Your Social Skills

Don't blow this one off in coping with your great loss. Many people damage their support system and discourage caregivers through unintentional disrespect and rudeness. Language skills are critical in how you address others and what you say to yourself. It may sound at first blush that social skills at your age (anyone over forty) are irrelevant. Nothing could be further from the truth. Your social skills are critical in the development of existing and much-needed new relationships. Too many people are at a loss for how to relate well in developing interpersonal relationships that assist in reinvesting in life. Make social skills and developing friendships your priorities. Here are some essentials to consider.

Begin with how you communicate, without which life withers. Do you address people by name? In a book published over a half century ago and still on the market, *How to Win Friends and Influence People*, author Dale Carnegie suggests that a person's name is the sweetest sound in the human language. An enthusiastic "Hello, Alice!" is much more meaningful than a low-key "Hi." Go back to **#81, Overcome the Constant Sense of Loneliness**, and reread the section on dealing with loneliness through the skillful use of validation.

Do you speak first when meeting contemporaries or strangers? This act alone can set the stage for positive interaction. Certainly there are strangers you might not want to engage, but overall, a simple hello can be a great icebreaker. Once a friendship begins, be careful about sharing too much too soon and appearing too needy. Take your time.

Smile. But not so fast, you may be thinking—who the hell feels like smiling? Put on a smile because it is a mood modifier and part of your downtime from grief. Smiling draws positive responses from those you interact with. It can easily be accomplished when you take your stress break or meet your best friend as starters. (Remember "fake it 'til you make it"?) Again, a hello with a captivating smile is simple to do and yet conveys a powerful nonverbal message. Make it a habit to break into a smile that makes the positive statement that you are glad to see the person.

Smiling is also a boost for your immune system and inner life, and is the best facial exercise for delaying aging signs. As a psychotherapist and colleague added: "Smiling also raises your spiritual vibrations and makes feeling the contact with your loved one easier and stronger."

Listen more than you talk. While your conversation is important, check to see if you are dominating the conversation. Ask a question or make a pleasant comment—then listen.

Become skilled at communicating symbolically and nonverbally. This is not hard to do. Language experts conclude that less than ten percent of verbal communication comes from the actual words we use. Voice inflection and body language (like a nod of understanding) account for the remainder of any message. When appropriate, give a hug or a kiss, a big wave, a tug on the arm, a pat on the shoulder, or a handshake.

Always keep in mind, that while first impressions count every time you meet someone, second and third impressions are just as important as the first. Boost and give your positive energy through body language. Project positive nonverbal clues such as upright posture, uncrossed arms, firm handshake, calm behavior, and focused attention as you squarely face the person. Consider your tone of voice when you answer or make a telephone call. Are you upbeat and pleasant, giving off positive vibes, or do you talk down and matter-of-fact in conversations?

Have you let your appearance go since your loved one died? Your neatness and apparel will always be important in friendships and in creating positive impressions. Don't dismiss this important element in developing social connections.

Become an expert at seeing things from someone else's perspective. Showing interest in what another likes is a great friend-maker. Learn to ask questions about their perspective or, as Carnegie suggests, "Talk in terms of the other person's interests." Don't jump to disagree until you have sufficient information and disagreement is essential. And by all means, when you don't understand a subject brought up, be willing to say, "I don't understand. Could you please explain that?"

Be generous with saying "thank you," as well as "I'm sorry" if you should have to apologize. This sensitivity is priceless. Be more than willing to acknowledge when you make a mistake. It can strengthen many relationships, since we all make plenty of mistakes and we can learn from them. A mistake is nothing more than having done something at the time that you felt was the correct thing to do, but turned out not to be the best choice.

Cut people some slack. We all make our mistakes. Avoid telling someone "You are wrong." Think about it: there are few things more damaging to the way you feel about someone than to hear these words directed to you. Find a kind way to disagree without wounding.

Be especially careful in the way you give and receive advice. Much conflict occurs due to the manner in which advice is handed out or taken. Be gentle and discreet. And keep in mind Samuel Taylor Coleridge's insight: "Advice is like snow—the softer it falls, the longer it dwells, and the deeper it sinks into the mind."

Finally, in developing the social skills essential for relationships that are guaranteed to bring peace of mind, practice the advice given by John Powell in a little book written decades ago titled *Why Am I Afraid to Tell You Who I Am?* "The genius of communication," he said, "is to be totally honest and totally kind at the same time." This is a lifelong project.

101. Never Stop Learning

Back in chapter 1, I said that one sure-fire way to cope with your loss is to learn all you can about the normalcy of the grief process. But don't stop there. Continue to keep your brain active by learning new things about your environment and the amazing world in which you live. Neuroscientists now tell us that we can generate new connections in the brain and help keep it healthy by giving it new challenges through learning. Additional connections are made, and neurons can be regenerated.

Find an interest, perhaps one you put on the back burner years ago or in childhood, and study all of the information presently available on it. Go to new places you haven't visited before. If you like to tour on cruise ships, consider taking a spiritual tour instead of a regular tour. You will not only go to exotic places, but you will be learning and focusing on your spiritual self as you strengthen beliefs. Try looking into Spirit Quest Tours.

Going to a new place doesn't have to be far away; it can be in your own town. Walk a different route or go to a store or a restaurant you haven't ever been to. Depending on your available time, make a pact with yourself that every week you will go to someplace in your county that you have never visited. Or try learning a skill you may need in the immediate future. Look up topics you have little knowledge of on the Internet.

All of this stimulation will not merely help your brain; it will take the focus off the constant dwelling on your loss. There are multiple advantages to widening your interests. You are in control of dealing with your loss and the constant changes that accompany it. At age ninety-nine, the famous heart surgeon Dr. Michael DeBakey said, "You can never learn enough." Use this advice as one of your long-term coping strategies as the weeks since the death of your loved one turn into months and years.

A Final Choice

As you have seen, there is a multiplicity of choices to be made in mourning, as well as in life. The choice of living again, finding joy, and landing back on your feet can be accomplished as you integrate your great loss into life. It is my hope that you will choose to keep building connections and the attitude that will bring you peace and love. Keep it up. You've come a long way. You will always remember your struggle, your loved one—and your success. Now I recommend in closing that you go back and reread **#9, Consciously Strive to Increase Your Ability to Love**, the greatest act of persistence you can ever perform—and live it with all your heart. Bless you all.

Helpful Books and Articles

Attig, Tom. *The Heart of Grief*. New York: Oxford University Press, 2000.

Baird, David. *Tranquil Thoughts on Love*. London: MQ Publications Limited, 2003.

Bissler, J. & Heiser, L. *Loving Connections: The Healing Power of After-Death Communications*. Createspace, 2008.

Brehony, Kathleen. *After the Darkest Hour: How Suffering Begins the Journey to Wisdom*. New York: Henry Holt & Company, 2000.

Browning, Sinclair. *Feathers Brush My Heart*. NY: Warner Books, 2002.

Carmody, Mitch. *Letters to My Son: Turning Loss to Legacy*. Edina, MN: Beaver Pond Press, 2011.

Connor, Pick. *Letting Go: The Grief Experience*. Carrollton, GA: AUM Productions, 1996.

Deits, Bob. *Life after Loss*. Tucson, AZ: Fisher Books, 1995.

Devers, Edie. *Goodbye Again: Experiences with Departed Loved Ones*. Kansas City: Andrews & McMeel, 1997.

Doka, Kenneth. (ed.) *Grief After Sudden Loss: Suicide, Accident, Heart Attack, Stroke:* Washington, D.C.: The Hospice Foundation of America, 1996.

Doka, Ken. *Living with Grief: Loss in Later Life*. Washington, DC: Hospice Foundation of America, 2002.

Duminiak, Christine. *Heaven Talks to Children*. New York: Citadel Press, Kensington Publishing Corporation, 2010.

Eliach, Yaffa. *Hasidic Tales of the Holocaust*. New York: Oxford University Press, 1982. (See pages 39–41, 169–172.)

Fenwick, P., et al. "Comfort for the Dying: Five Year Retrospective and One Year Prospective Studies of End of Life Experiences." *Archives of Gerontology and Geriatrics* (2009), doi:10.1016/j.archger.2009.10.004.

Finley, Mitch. *Whispers of Love: Encounters with Deceased Relatives and Friends*. New York: Crossroads, 1995.

Fitzgerald, Helen. *The Mourning Handbook*. New York: Simon & Schuster, 1995.

Guggenheim, W. & Guggenheim, J. *Hello from Heaven*. New York: Bantam, 1996.

Haraldsson, Erlendur. "The Iyengar-Kirti Case: An Apparitional Case of the Bystander Type." *Journal of the Society for Psychical Research* (1987) 54, No. 806.

Horsley, Gloria, & Horsley, Heidi. *Hope: Inspirational Stories of Healing After Loss*. Palo Alto, CA: Open to Hope Foundation, 2011.

Howell, Edward. *Connect: 12 Vital Ties that Open Your Heart, Lengthen Your Life, and Deepen Your Soul.* New York: Pocket Books, 1999.

Inglis, Brian. *Coincidences: A Matter of Chance—Or Synchronicity?* London: Hutchinson, 1990.

Jeffers, Susan. *Embracing Uncertainty: Breakthrough Methods for Achieving Peace of Mind When Facing the Unknown.* New York: St. Martin's Press, 2003.

Kastenbaum, Robert. *Is There Life after Death?* London: Multimedia Books Limited, 1995. (See pages 90–96.)

Kubler-Ross, E. *Death Is of Vital Importance.* Barrytown, NY: Station Hill Press, 1995. (See pages 95–98.)

Kubler-Ross, Elisabeth & Kessler, David. *On Grief and Grieving.* New York: Scribner, 2005.

Kushner, Harold. *When Bad Things Happen to Good People.* New York: Knopf Doubleday, 2004.

LaGrand, Louis. *Four Key Questions to Ask Yourself When Mourning.* www.ezinearticles.com, July 2011.

LaGrand, L. "Releasing Emotional Pain When Grieving." *Hospice Volunteer News: An e-Magazine Published by the Hospice Volunteer Association*, Spring 2009.

———. "Grief, Loss, and Brain Maintenance." *Open to Hope Foundation*, February 2009.

———. "An Extraordinary Experience that Eased the Burden of Grief." *Midwest Caregiver*, January 2009, 30.

———. "Using Extraordinary Experiences to Cope with the Death of a Loved One." *Hospice Volunteer News: An e-Magazine Published by the Hospice Volunteer Association*, Spring 2008.

———. "The Secret Life of the Bereaved." *The Journal of Spirituality and Paranormal Studies*, November 2007.

———. *Love Lives On: Learning from the Extraordinary Encounter of the Bereaved*. New York: Berkley Books, 2006.

———. "Incorporating the Extraordinary Experiences of the Bereaved into Personal Rituals." *The Forum*, Oct./Nov./Dec. 2005.

———. "The Nature and Therapeutic Implications of the Extraordinary Experiences of the Bereaved." *Journal of Near-Death Studies*, 24(1), Fall 2005, 3-20.

———. *Gifts from the Unknown*. New York: Authors Choice Press, 2001.

———. *Messages and Miracles: Extraordinary Experiences of the Bereaved*. St. Paul, MN: Llewellyn Publications, 1999.

———. *After-Death Communication: Final Farewells*. St. Paul, MN: Llewellyn Publications, 1997.

———. "Are We Missing Opportunities to Help the Bereaved?" *The Forum*, Vol. 23 (September/October 1997): 5.

Lewis, C. S. *A Grief Observed*. New York: Bantam, 1980. (See pages 85–87.)

Moore, Thomas. *Dark Nights of the Soul: A Guide for Finding Your Way through Life's Ordeals*. New York: Gotham Books, 2005.

More, T. *Care of the Soul*. New York: Harper Perennial, 1994.

Morrell, D. *Fireflies*. New York: E. P. Dutton, 1988. (See pages 33–47.)

Radin, Dean. *The Conscious Universe: The Scientific Truth of Psychic Phenomena*. San Francisco: Harper Edge, 1997.

Smith, Harold Ivan. *ABCs of Healthy Grieving: A Companion for Everyday Coping*. 2nd ed., Notre Dame, IN: Ave Maria Press, 2007.

Smith, Harold Ivan. *A Decembered Grief: Living with Loss While Others Are Celebrating*. Kansas City: Beacon Hill, 1999

Sparrow, Scott. *I Am with You Always*. New York: Bantam, 1995.

Steffen, E. & Coyle, A. "Can 'sense of presence' experiences in bereavement be conceptualized as spiritual phenomena?" *Mental Health, Religion & Culture*, 2010, 13, 273–291.

Summit-Riker, Jean. *Forever Is Still a Long, Long Time*. Patchogue, NY: Stardust Publishing Company, 2010.

Treece, Patricia. *Messengers: After-Death Appearances of Saints and Mystics*. Huntington, IN: Our Sunday Visitor Publishing Division, 1995.

Varga, Josie. *Visits from Heaven*. Virginia Beach, VA: A.R.E. Press, 2009.

Wolfelt, Alan. *Journey through Grief*. Fort Collins, CO: Companion Press, 1997.

About the Author

Louis E. LaGrand, PhD., has been an expert in the field of bereavement for over thirty years. He is Distinguished Service Professor Emeritus at the State University of New York and Adjunct Professor of Health Careers at the Eastern Campus of Suffolk Community College in Riverhead, New York. He is former member of the Board of Directors of the Association for Death Education and Counseling, and he is known world-wide for his grief research on the Extraordinary Experiences of the bereaved. He holds advanced degrees from Columbia University, the University of Notre Dame, and Florida State. He gives seminars and workshops on death-related topics in schools, hospices, and health agencies in the US, Canada, and England.

He is currently Bereavement Coordinator at Our Lady of Lourdes Church in Venice, Florida, where he directs support groups for widows and widowers, and is Director of Loss Education Associates, a grief education resource that features Dr. LaGrand as a seminar and workshop presenter.

Dr. LaGrand is also a bereavement columnist for the quarterly print publication of the Hospice Volunteer Association, which facilitates and supports a global volunteer community committed to providing the most compassionate service possible to those who are dying and their bereaved.